Better Homes and Gardens®
flea market
decorating

Meredith® Books
Des Moines, Iowa

Better Homes and Gardens® Books
An imprint of Meredith® Books

Flea Market Decorating
Editor: Vicki L. Ingham
Art Director: Ken Carlson
Principal Photographer: Bill Holt
Contributing Editors: Heather Lobdell, Trish Maharam, Hillary Maharam,
    Elaine Markoutsas, Eleanor Roper, Mary Anne Thomson
Copy Chief: Catherine Hamrick
Copy and Production Editor: Terri Fredrickson
Contributing Copy Editor: Carol Boker
Contributing Proofreaders: Nancy Dietz, Judy Friedman, Beth Popplewell
Electronic Production Coordinator: Paula Forest
Editorial and Design Assistants: Kaye Chabot, Mary Lee Gavin, Karen Schirm
Production Director: Douglas M. Johnston
Book Production Managers: Pam Kvitne, Marjorie J. Schenkelberg

Meredith® Books
Editor in Chief: James D. Blume
Design Director: Matt Strelecki
Managing Editor: Gregory H. Kayko
Executive Shelter Editor: Denise L. Caringer

Director, Sales & Marketing, Retail: Michael A. Peterson
Director, Sales & Marketing, Special Markets: Rita McMullen
Director, Sales & Marketing, Home & Garden Center Channel: Ray Wolf
Director, Operations: George A. Susral

Vice President, General Manager: Jamie L. Martin

Better Homes and Gardens® Magazine
Editor in Chief: Jean LemMon
Executive Interior Design Editor: Sandra S. Soria

Meredith Publishing Group
President, Publishing Group: Christopher M. Little
Vice President, Consumer Marketing & Development: Hal Oringer

Meredith Corporation
Chairman and Chief Executive Officer: William T. Kerr

Chairman of the Executive Committee: E. T. Meredith III

All of us at Better Homes and Gardens® Books are dedicated to providing you with information and ideas to enhance your home. We welcome your comments and suggestions. Write to us at: Better Homes and Gardens Books, Shelter Editorial Department, 1716 Locust St., Des Moines, IA 50309-3023.

If you would like to purchase any of our books, check wherever quality books are sold. Visit us at bhg.com or bhgbooks.com.

table of contents

introduction

adventures in decorating

For many people, the irresistible allure of seasonal antiques fairs and flea markets lies in the passion for collecting a particular type of object, whether it's green bowls, cast-iron toys, or picture frames. For me, the anticipation I feel as I approach a field full of tents also has to do with the hope of finding treasure— the unique, the singular, something wacky, weathered, or wonderful that I can take home and put to use. Even though I hope I'll get it for a good price, it's more important that it speak to me because it has acquired a patina of use, its worn surface conveying age, roots, a past life. If it can serve some new function other than the one for which it was intended, so much the better. Cast-iron tub feet make great bookends. An orchard ladder holds fresh towels nicely. Metal claw-and-ball legs from a piano stool easily become finials for a do-it-yourself drapery rod.

Seeing objects out of context and finding new uses for them turns decorating into a creative adventure. It's fun to solve an ordinary problem in an extraordinary way, whether it's turning a washtub into a fountain, metal boxes into file drawers, or doorknobs into curtain tiebacks. And the look that results is distinctively personal. This book isn't about collecting the next hot item. It's about using the things you discover at flea markets, antiques fairs, and yard sales to decorate your home in a way that expresses your own personality, interests, and sense of style. While you may not be able to reproduce the ideas in this book exactly—since flea market finds are often one of a kind—I hope you'll see ways you can adapt and reuse similar kinds of items. I also hope you'll find inspiration to look at everything with a fresh eye for its creative potential to become something else.

Vicki Ingham

the hunt

The call is compelling: Somewhere in the acres of booths and piles of junk awaits a treasure with your name on it. True, the likelihood is slim that you'll find an original Tiffany lamp at a bargain-basement price. The real excitement lies in searching for objects with presence that bring distinctive character to your home.

finders keepers

flea markets and outdoor antiques fairs were once the well-kept secrets of antiques dealers and interior designers, but no more. As a recreational shopping experience that promises the adventure of the hunt and the satisfaction of thrift, flea markets attract people of all ages, tastes, and income levels.

Some antiques dealers complain that it's getting harder to find good deals at flea markets now, and tables of tube socks and discount detergents often replace antiques and collectibles. You still can count on finding a variety of objects of all kinds at large seasonal antiques shows, but don't overlook yard or garage sales, estate sales, and thrift stores, such as those operated by Goodwill or the Salvation Army. These may be the most promising places to find the best bargains because the vendors are handling a wide variety of merchandise and may not realize what

Agricultural artifacts are popular at flea markets because they have country cachet but can serve new functions. Fill a wire basket like this with magazines or cassette tapes, or line it with moss and insert a pot of flowers.

HENS LAY MORE WITH

MASTER MIX FEEDS

EGGLAC PELLETS

1 American art pottery has become highly collectible—and pricey. Study price guides so you can make informed purchases.

2 Although this temple doll was purchased at a flea market in Japan (see the story on pages 40–47), you may find items from around the world at any market, as people clean out closets and recycle souvenirs.

Dress for success—casually and comfortably. Wear good walking shoes and leave the

they have. If you like to make antiquing part of your vacation plans, see the list of fairs on pages 214–20.

what to wear

At outdoor antiques fairs and flea markets, a lot of the merchandise will be covered with dust and grime. So dress comfortably in clothes and shoes you won't mind getting dirty. If shows are set up at fairgrounds or in fields, the area may be muddy or dusty, depending on the weather. At the beginning and end of the flea market season, when a day can start off chilly and warm up fast, it's a good idea to dress in layers. Also remember to apply sunscreen; even on a hazy day, you can end up with a painful sunburn after hours of looking at tables laden with wares.

what to bring

Leave the heavy purse at home and carry the essentials in a fanny pack or backpack. Some dealers will accept personal checks, but don't expect to use a credit card. If you have cash, especially plenty of small bills, the dealer may give a better discount on prices. Also, if you're likely to get carried away, bringing cash will help you control your spending.

If you're looking for a piece of furniture to fit a particular spot, bring the measurements with you on a notepad. (In fact, some people carry their room measurements with them at all times, in case they come across an unexpected treasure.) The notepad also will come in handy for recording

expensive jewelry and heavy handbag at home; do bring sunscreen.

your expenditures and the locations of booths where you leave large or heavy purchases to pick up later. Bring a tape measure to check the dimensions of furniture and picture frames. (In a pinch, you can use a dollar bill—it's 6 inches long.) A magnet helps you identify metals (brass and copper

2

won't hold a magnet, but iron and steel will). If you're collecting china, silver, or pewter, a small magnifying glass helps you to read hallmarks more easily; it also can help you determine whether the chipped carving on a picture frame is molded resin, gesso, or carved wood. (Resin looks like translucent plastic and is less valuable than the other two.)

If you're an avid collector of a specific item, you may want to bring along a price guide, but if you're just looking for interesting pieces that can serve creative new purposes at home, there's no need. It's a good idea to bring a bottle of

❶ Japanese glass fishing weights are free on the beach in the Northwest, but they're a flea market prize on the East Coast. **❷** Your first response to finding an old fencing mask might be to try it on—but could it be turned into a wall lamp?

water and some moist towelettes (your hands can get very grubby handling rusted iron and dusty wood). Most outdoor markets have snacks and fast food, and a packed lunch is just one more thing to carry. Stuff some plastic or paper bags in your backpack, in case vendors don't have any, and consider taking a cart or wagon to carry smaller pieces as you go through the market. Finally, keep an old blanket, some bubble wrap, and bungee cords in the car so you can transport your treasures home safely.

❸ Orbs of all kinds, from croquet balls to stone lawn balls to glass fishing weights, are popular as decorative accents to display in wire or woven baskets.

when to arrive

Conventional wisdom dictates that you arrive as soon as the gates open in the morning (or up to an hour and a half before) to get the best choice of goods. (Another benefit is you'll claim a close parking place.) This advice suggests that dealers sweep in before dawn as vendors are still unloading their trucks and snatch up all the best stuff before the nonprofessional shoppers get to see it. This can cause some competitive-shopping anxiety if your goal is to find "the best stuff," too—but relax. Shopping at flea markets is an exercise in creativity, and that cast-iron fireplace insert that the dealer passed up can become the perfect tub-side table or garden accent you need at home.

Some experienced shoppers find that arriving later in the day (around 2 p.m. or 3 p.m.) gets them better prices on items vendors don't want to pack up and take home. But beware: If the weather is bad or if vendors have done well, they may begin packing up by noon. And if you arrive one-half hour before closing time, all you'll see is promising pieces being put back in the truck.

how to shop

Should you browse slowly from booth to booth, or whip through briskly, scanning tables and stopping only when something extraordinary catches your eye? It depends. If you're a serious collector of green bowls or you're only looking for

Buy for love, not money—antiques and collectibles are meant to be used and enjoyed.

1930s quilts, then the zoom-and-scan approach works best. Some longtime flea market shoppers advocate walking through the whole show quickly to get a feeling for which dealers carry similar items. It can pay to compare goods and prices because dealers may price their wares differently.

If you're new to flea markets—or if you're just looking for anything interesting that might come in handy—relax and enjoy yourself. Explore the booths that appeal to

① Use a notepad to keep track of purchases and of booths where you leave items to retrieve later. ② Test a chair for sturdiness by pressing down on the seat and arms. You can reglue wobbly joints, but broken legs will be difficult to fix.

Trying to cash in on the next hot collectible is about as risky as investing in junk bonds.

2

1 Antique sconces that you can use with candles or wire for electric bulbs are good flea market buys. If you like the rusted look, apply paste wax or linseed oil to enhance the color. **2** Are these candlesticks new or old? Dealers like to share what they know, so don't hesitate to ask questions.

Rust and peeling paint lend charm, but if you have small children, avoid pieces with

1

you, and keep your eyes open for an intriguing piece that could serve some purpose other than the one for which it was intended. Ask yourself: What can I put in it? What can I put on it? Where could I hang it? What else could I do with it besides use it for its original purpose?

Once you've found something you like, evaluate its condition. A little rust on metal or peeling paint on wood adds to the object's charm. If veneer is missing or a chair leg is broken, however, repairs may be more costly or time-consuming than they're worth (see pages 196–213 for tips on assessing condition). You can reglue a chair that's in pieces if the pieces aren't broken, but such a job requires time, patience, and carpentry skills. If you find an upholstered piece you like, give it the sniff test: You may find it impossible to remove tobacco or pet odors or a musty, mildewy smell. If you like a sofa's shape and want to reupholster it, remember that it takes at least 12 yards of fabric for reupholstery, plus $750 or more for labor. That can become a good investment if the sofa is one you'll want to live with for a long time.

Also consider whether you can use an imperfect item as is, or use parts of it. A chipped sugar bowl can hold flowers; a teapot without its lid can

flaking paint. Old paint is likely to contain lead, a toxic substance when ingested.

do the same. You can cut up torn or stained tablecloths or bedspreads to make pillows, stuffed toys, or even clothing.

how to buy

Unless an item is marked "firm," it's okay to haggle—but politely. Asking "Is this your best price?" or "Could you do better on this price for me?" usually prompts the dealer to take 5 to 10 percent off the marked price. You can make a counteroffer ("Would you take X amount?"), but don't insult

❷

1 Check trunk locks for signs of wear to make sure they're as old as the trunk. **2** Display a school of fishing lures as a rustic collection, or consider mounting a few along the top of an old chair for folk-art whimsy. **3** The Anchor Hocking Glass Corporation began making Fire King glass ovenware in the 1940s. The light green color, called Jadeite, is particularly collectible now.

the dealer by making your counteroffer drastically lower, especially if the price is clearly reasonable. Often, you can get a better deal if you offer to buy two or three things from the same booth. If a piece is unmarked, ask the price rather than offering one of your own, then counteroffer if you like. Never complain about having seen the same item for less somewhere else and don't insult the vendor's knowledge or merchandise. If the price is still more than you want to pay or if you have doubts, walk away and think about it. But remember that someone else may snatch it up while you're thinking. If you love it and the price is one you're willing to pay, buy it. Beauty is in the eye of the beholder, and if it's worth the money to you, that's what counts.

other venues

You can take the same friendly approach to bargaining—asking "Is this price firm?" or "Is this your best price?"—at garage sales, estate sales, and in many antiques stores. Thrift shops run by charitable organizations, on the other hand, have low prices to begin with and the proceeds go to charity, so haggling would not be appropriate.

shopping in cyberspace

eBay, at ebay.com (see sample screen shots below and page 23, top), offers millions of items on a site that's very easy to use.

eHammer, at ehammer.com (see page 23 bottom), auctions a broad range of art, antiques, and collectibles and offers escrow services.

Online auction sites aren't likely to replace flea markets, but they're worth investigating if you're searching for specific collectibles or types of merchandise.

You'll need a computer and a modem with at least a 28.8 speed (56.6 is preferred). You also will need access to the Internet, which you can obtain by subscribing to a service such as America Online, Prodigy, or CompuServe; or you can sign up with a local Internet provider and use a browser such as Netscape Navigator or Microsoft Internet Explorer. (Most new computers come with one of these already loaded.)

To access online auction sites, type the World Wide Web address in the bar at the top of the screen and hit the "enter" key; or choose a search engine such as Excite, Google, or AltaVista™ and type in "antiques" or "flea markets." Hundreds of listings will appear; if you find a site you like, be sure to bookmark it so you can return to it easily.

Once you find an auction featuring the kinds of items that interest you, read the auction rules carefully. Some have tutorials that guide you through the process. Generally, you'll find a description of each item, a starting price or the current price, the number of bids posted, and the time and date that the bidding closes. Read the descriptions closely; items are offered "as is," although some sites may let you return an item within a limited amount of time. The seller's e-mail address may be provided so you can contact him or her directly with questions about the condition of a piece. Many online auction houses have a feedback site that lets you check on other buyers' experiences with the seller. Remember that although it's in

the seller's best interest to be honest and forthcoming—and most are—buying antiques online involves some risk, and you may have a hard time proving you didn't receive what you paid for.

To place a bid, you'll have to register with the online auction house to receive a user ID and a password. Then type in the maximum amount you're willing to pay. The auction house takes it from there, bidding by proxy for you. Once you place a bid, it's considered a binding contract, and you won't be allowed to retract it except under special conditions. If your bid is accepted, most auction houses will notify you by e-mail, and it will be up to you and the seller to arrange for payment and shipping. You will have to pay taxes, shipping, and insurance, and you also may be charged a buyer's fee of up to 10 percent, so be sure to read all of the rules before you begin bidding. Pay by check or credit card, never cash. Some auction houses have escrow arrangements that protect both the buyer and the seller by holding your money until you receive the item and declare yourself satisfied. Fees for this service can run up to $45 for a $1,000 purchase, but you may be able to negotiate with the seller to pay all or part of the amount.

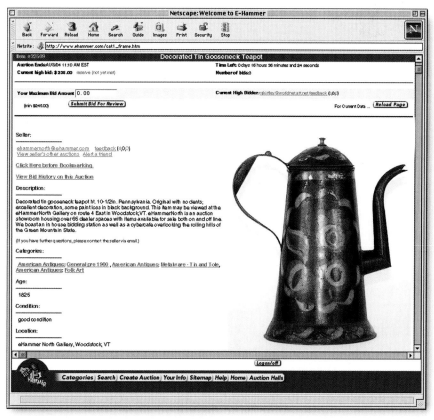

defining a style

The pleasure—and point—of decorating with flea market finds and thrift shop treasures is to create a look that's distinctively your own. On the following pages, you'll see how eight homeowners choose and combine flea market finds to assemble rooms filled with character. Use their styles as inspiration to help you identify ways you'd like to express your own personality through objects, colors, and textures that appeal to you.

salvage chic

jeff Jones bought his first piece of architectural salvage—a pine stair baluster—when he was 17 or 18 years old. "I went to visit an aunt in Louisville, Kentucky, and found it in an antiques store. It was affordable, so I bought it." After college, he made his first flea market buy, a stack of old leather suitcases that still serves as a handy side table in the living room. Both purchases showed foresight: After a detour into advertising and graphic design, Jeff became an architect and an antiques dealer known for his creative ability to put old objects to new uses. His home in Midtown Atlanta showcases both talents, incorporating salvaged and "repurposed" materials into both the structure and furnishings. The result feels rooted in tradition but lightened with a fresh, modern sensibility.

creative reuse

Seeing new possibilities for old objects is an intuitive process for Jeff. "It has to hit me when I see it. Some things I love, and I'm constantly asking myself what I can

Jeff Jones mixes antiques, such as the 18th-century Greek oil jars in the living room, with more humble flea market finds to create a look that's rooted in classical tradition.

do with them. But if it's not really clear up front, I usually don't do anything."

In the living room, an old luggage cart from the Atlanta train station serves as a coffee table. On it, an English garden cloche rests upside down in an old metal light fixture (also upside down). The large glass bell-shaped jars were originally placed over seedlings in the garden to protect them from late frosts. "I'd seen the cloches at antiques shows," says Jeff, "and a dealer friend had this one sitting upside down in her shop. I saw it and immediately thought 'candles,' and nabbed it. I've since seen them everywhere, used for planters or holding all kinds of things."

found sculpture

Sometimes an object's new function is purely aesthetic. Jeff's chunky pine baluster simply stands as sculpture, as does a rare, French antique terra-cotta acanthus-leaf finial on the coffee table. The red brass-mounted box on the coffee table once held engineering tools. It still could provide storage in its velvet-lined interior,

---

Salvaged bricks were handpicked for the fireplace, chosen for the remnants of paint on them. The mantelpiece features an antique overdoor panel.

1

Almost anything can become a lamp. Jeff found surveyors' tripods in an antiques

but it serves a primarily decorative function here, providing height for a more interesting table display.

designer lamps

As an antiques dealer, Jeff was known for the lamps he made from unexpected objects. Almost anything was—and is—fair game: a surveyor's tripod has the right height and scale for a floor lamp; an andiron takes on a quirky, Oriental quality as a dresser lamp. The cast-iron base of a Villager dress form crouches on the bedside table (see page 36), and a 17th-century sandstone sculpture fragment provides a base for a slender accent light in the living room (see page 27).

Jeff usually assembles the lamps himself so he can make sure the fittings, finials, and shades have the right proportions. Also, he says, "you have to figure it out as you go along." To drill the hole for the fitting on the sandstone sculpture fragment, he used a hand drill, but more often he uses an overhead drill press to make sure the shaft is perfectly vertical. To ensure that the shades are as distinctive as the bases, and in scale with them, he shops for old lampshade frames that he can strip down and recover; or he has shades custom-made.

lateral thinking

Jeff says the secret to his approach is lateral thinking. "Sometimes you have to come at things from a different point of view or through the back door," he says.

shop in Colorado and thought they would make good floor lamps.

"Try to think of other sources for items or other ways to solve a problem." Once, not long after he had bought the curvaceous armchair on page 28, he was having a leather coat made. "It hit me that the olive-colored leather for the coat would be perfect on the chair," he says, so he persuaded

❶ Jeff assembles and wires his lamps himself, but you also could have a lamp shop do it for you. If new lampshades aren't in scale with your lamp, look for old frames that you can strip and recover. **❷** This andiron already had a hole in the center to receive the lamp fitting.

❷

the shop owner to sell him a few extra yards at a good price. In the same way, instead of investing in cotton duck or twill for slipcovers, Jeff goes to a home improvement center and buys a few painters' drop cloths. It gives the same effect for one-third the cost of upholstery fabric.

In the bedroom, he says, "I decided I wanted a four-poster bed but with a different scale, and I didn't want the usual four-poster." He came across a set of game sticks and balls that appealed to him. "A client of mine was collecting balls, and I kept thinking about them," he says, "and then it hit me what the sticks could be." He had a metal bed frame made to hold the box spring and mattress and had sockets welded to the corners of the frame to hold the game sticks (see page 37). A fifth game stick with its color-coordinated wooden ball hangs on the wall as art.

Although Jeff does some of the work himself in repurposing objects, jobs that involve welding metal or cutting marble call for specialists. That's when he

To solve decorating problems creatively, look for materials and objects that everyone

turns to contacts made during his 20-year career as an architect and then an antiques dealer. Finding someone in your area to handle similar jobs may take some telephone work. Start with the Yellow Pages and look under "machine shops" or "welding" for metalwork.

1 Sections of an old iron fence have been welded to make the patio table. **2** Although antique oil jars like this one are now hard to come by, their classical shapes continue to inspire good reproductions. **3** A wax boudoir-doll head dating from 1880 to 1920 stands as sculpture on a stack of suitcases.

else has overlooked and ask yourself what other purposes they can serve.

3

1 A tie bolt from a church in Brooklyn, New York, looks like modern sculpture on the dining room wall. Iron brackets from an old fence support the kitchen mantel, which displays a wooden mold for making steel cogs. **2** A vintage sign hangs over the stainless-steel kitchen island.

1

Jeff opened his antiques shop as a way of "taking a rest" from an architectural practice that included designing nursing homes, international hotels, and commercial interiors—among them the offices for the 1996 Olympics in Atlanta. Now he's going back to architecture, renovating old buildings and designing retail and residential interiors.

Although he doesn't espouse a particular style, he does have a signature way of working with older materials to give settings a feeling of age. He describes his own home as "old-world flair with a zing to it." He appreciates old things but pays attention to balancing them with something new. "I aim to have contrasts in materials, contrasts of old and new," he says, "so the results don't look like a period reproduction."

building character

Jeff's own house illustrates his approach. He and his partner, Mike Boykin, had planned to buy and convert a vintage duplex into a single residence, but the plan fell through. So Jeff took the duplex's mirror-image floor plan, with rooms arranged symmetrically along a central corridor, and enlarged it to fit a lot in another old neighborhood. "The exterior is an exact duplicate of that little house," says Jeff. For the interior, he and Mike collected bricks, wood, and architectural pieces for

about a year. The wooden floors came from factories all over the Northeast. To find the bricks for the twin fireplaces that serve all four front rooms, they located a salvage yard in Atlanta and sorted through piles of old bricks to find the ones that still had paint on them. The mantels in the living room and dining room were made from weathered wood and embellished with antique French and English decorative overdoor moldings. All of the paneled interior doors came from old houses in the area. Because builders don't like to hang old doors, Jeff had to have frames constructed and the doors pre-hung so they could be popped in place as units.

"We collected a lot of stuff before we broke ground," says Jeff. He then adjusted the design of the house to incorporate the pieces. The cabinet doors in the kitchen and bathroom are 200-year-old interior window shutters from a house in Pennsylvania. Jeff says, "I wasn't sure how or whether I'd use them, but I grabbed them anyway." To convert them into cabinet doors, he had the cabinets built as boxes to fit the shutters. In the master bath, where twin sinks are tucked under windows overlooking the back porch, Jeff had mirrors mounted inside the shutter doors so light and views are unobstructed.

Where there's a will, there's usually a way. A lamp shop can help you wire an object to

For the master bath lavatory, Jeff had a metalworker weld together sections of old iron fencing to make a console base; holes cut into the marble top receive the bowl-shape sinks. In the guest bath, Jeff mounted porcelain faucet handles on the

②

① The cast-iron base of the bedside lamp was the base of a Villager dress form.

② Sticks and balls from a European game serve as posts on the bed. Jeff had sockets welded to the bed frame to hold the sticks. The balls are wired in place.

turn it into a lamp. A machine shop can weld items together for you.

Vintage faucet handles make unusual towel holders in the bathroom. You also could use

wall as towel holders. "I've learned since that you have to buy
the ones that come in two pieces, so you can disassemble them,
insert a screw, and reassemble them.

"A lot of things you look at aren't as easy to convert [to other
purposes] as you'd think," he cautions. "But be open to a piece,
and if you love it, get it, even if all you do is set it in a corner."

1 The 200-year-old shutters conceal a medicine cabinet and mirrors. New sinks set into marble rest on vintage fencing.

2 Old porcelain faucet handles make ingenious towel holders. Look for ones with stems that can be disassembled so you can insert a screw, reassemble the stem, and then insert the screw into the wall. A large washer serves as a faceplate and gives a finished look.

doorknobs and mount them on a strip of wood installed under a shelf.

flavor european

barbara Novogratz doesn't let language get in the way when she shops flea markets in Europe and Asia. Her secret? "Just learn the exchange rate and how to say thank you, and you can make it," she says. Barbara successfully negotiates purchases abroad by asking the dealer to write down a price on her notepad. She then calculates the exchange rate in her head and writes down a counteroffer. In Japan, her shopping savvy netted 18 temple dolls that date to 1900 for about $3 each. "The matched sets are very expensive. Families put them up for holidays honoring the emperor. But mismatched or leftover dolls can be very cheap." Be careful when you make an offer, cautions Barbara. In Paris, if it's too low, you may insult the vendors, and they won't sell to you at any price.

family flea marketing

Barbara began going to flea markets and country auctions as a young military wife. "I had a baby on one hip and one in the stroller," she says. "I'd take

A tall-case clock from England stands beside the bay window, where Barbara Novogratz displays an antique hobby horse she found in a French flea market.

1 Iron fencing from a Charleston widow's walk serves as a fire screen. The wooden flame on the hearth was a guild symbol for firefighters in northern Germany. **2** Barbara uses Japanese temple dolls as place markers for dinner parties.

popcorn and bananas to keep them busy while I shopped." Her hobby became a business as she sold pieces to buy better ones. "My children say they were the only kids they knew who could go to school and come home to find all of their furniture gone," she says.

euro flea

Many of the pieces that furnish the Novogratz home today came from flea markets in Germany when military duty took the family there in the mid-1980s. One of the couple's best finds was the painted wedding chest that serves as a coffee table in the living room. "It was covered with brown paint, but it had bun

1 A Victorian iron garden chair holds fresh towels in the bathroom.

2 A steel dentist's cabinet stores toiletries. Storage pieces like this are good investments because you can use them in more than one room.

1

If a shop owner isn't ready to part with a display piece that you long to buy, leave your

2

name and number and a price you'd be willing to pay. You may get a call weeks later.

1 Barbara mounted a
Victorian overmantel on the
wall to serve as a display
shelf. To snag a prize like the
painted bed, she arrives
before the market opens,
while dealers are still
unpacking. **2** On her porch,
a small pavilion displays
potted flowers. Barbara
found the pavilion at a yard
sale, mounted on a pole and
holding a bowl of birdseed.

feet and good lines and only cost $100, so we took it to an antiques restorer to have him paint it in the old style. When he removed some of the brown paint, he found the original 1827 painted design underneath."

Barbara constantly searches for unusual pieces to stock the space she rents at Twig House, an antiques shop in Vienna, Virginia. Like most dealers, she usually doesn't become permanently attached to her finds, but that can have its drawbacks. "My problem is, I'll get tired of things and sell them, and then I never can find anything like them again!"

cottage style

Cathlene (C. J.) VanDaff usually dresses her mantel formally, with topiaries and Chinese porcelain ducks flanking a 19th-century painting of kittens. For purposes of photography, however, and in the spirit of celebrating a successful day at the Allegan Antiques Market, she created this collage of flea market finds. The graphic arrangement of picture frames, wooden spindles, an iron bracket, and a wire trivet reflects the interior designer's eye for composition. The objects also capture her affinity for weathered textures and time-softened colors that convey a sense of age and long use. In her 1930s East Grand Rapids cottage, C. J. combines painted furniture with old wicker and antique reupholstered pieces to create rooms that are cozy, comfortable, and stylish.

color cues

As a clean, sun-washed backdrop for her romantic mix of furnishings and accessories, C. J. chose a soft butter yellow for the walls and crisp white for the

The mantel offers a lesson in composition: Overlapping picture frames carve out negative spaces of different sizes. Contrasting shapes—a round trivet and a triangular bracket—rest on the frames' edges, and candlesticks enclose the arrangement.

trim. The yellow was inspired by her collection of 19th-century Staffordshire and majolica, which she began collecting when she was at Kendall College of Art and Design studying interior design. "Majolica was the Victorian poor person's pottery," she says. "It was imprinted with leaves and painted with garden colors that lean to soft pastels." Over the last decade, it has become highly collectible. C. J. bought her first piece, a begonia-leaf dish, for $8 in the mid-1980s. "Today it's worth at least $150," she says.

She displays much of her collection in a 19th-century painted cupboard that was found in an old barn. The cupboard's simple, straight lines contrast with the refined, graceful shapes of French-style bergère chairs, which C. J. upholstered in a floral and plaid. Mixing formal pieces like these with more primitive ones produces a stylish, sophisticated comfort—and you'd never guess that the wicker chair was a $40 find and the needlepoint rug a $25 bargain. "Antiquing requires a little more creativity than walking into a furniture store and taking Living Room Set Number One," she says. "The things you get at a flea market are one of a kind. They are unique." They also can offer an affordable way to furnish your home.

1 C. J. VanDaff's majolica collection inspired the choice of yellow for her walls. The primitive cupboard was languishing in a barn; she had picture lights installed to highlight her collection.
2 Large and small nail barrels serve as side tables in the den. A large wire basket of unknown origin holds magazines, and old shutters create a cozy feeling of enclosure.

As an interior designer, C. J. has access to dozens of sources for fabrics, furniture, hardware, rugs, and art. For singular items with character, however, she still turns to the dusty (or muddy) fields of flea markets, where she can spot a treasure and strike a bargain. Her love of "the hunt" started with garage sales when C. J. was furnishing her first home. "When you're furnishing on a budget, it's a wonderful way to go," says C. J. "You start thinking of adaptive reuses—using a picnic basket for big plants to fill a corner, for example." In her den, C. J. uses old barrels as side tables and a big wire basket as a magazine rack. She also turns porch spindles into lamps and candlesticks.

advice from a pro

C. J.'s advice for successful flea marketing:

Buy what you love, what you respond to with a passion. "I don't have things out that I don't love," says C. J.

Be open to possibilities, but decide what you can live with. Are you looking for something in mint condition, or can you live with

Buy what you love and you'll find a place to use it. Decorating with flea market finds

imperfections? Not everyone is comfortable with peeling paint and rust.

Be impulsive. Decide on the spot—but base your final price on a limit that you set for yourself. Don't buy something because you think it will increase in value. It may, but that's a bonus.

Weigh your decision with logic. It's good to take someone whose opinion you trust as a practical sounding board.

Decorating with flea market finds has influenced C. J.'s design style. "It draws your eye to look at things in new ways, to be more

C. J. mixes antique linens and easy-care, vintage-look new bedding to dress the bed. To match the old picket fence that serves as the headboard, her brother built a matching picket fence around the stairwell leading to the attic bedroom.

"draws the eye to look at things in new ways, to be more creative," says C. J. VanDaff.

creative," she says. She credits both of her parents for the creativity they passed along and says her Dutch heritage plays a part, too.

"In our house, many things were handmade and homemade. It was an economic consideration, but also, it was full of love." She finds the same kind of heart in vintage fabrics and accessories, in their power to evoke a feeling of comfort and a sense of tradition.

❶ A sugar bowl with a missing lid works well as a flowerpot. ❷ A group of small mirrors reflects light to enhance the feeling of space in the bathroom. A mannequin hand makes a whimsical soap dish.

retro
rustic

Staying in the guest cottage at Mary Anne and Tom Thomson's weekend home in Clarksville, Missouri, is like stepping back in time. "I have a reproduction of an old radio in the cottage," says Mary Anne, "and I have tapes of '40s music. When people come in from out of town, they're stressed. When they walk into a place with no phone, no TV, and Billie Holiday playing on the radio, they enter another world. Their blood pressure drops 20 points." Instead of playing computer games or watching videos, guests can entertain themselves by leafing through stacks of old movie magazines, cowboy magazines, and old issues of *Life*. "People love it," she says.

an evolved look

Mary Anne collected most of the furnishings and accessories for the cottage from antiques shops, garage sales, and flea markets around the little river town. "I wanted to furnish the cottage with things that were indestructible, so guests could relax and not worry about it," she says. "I've always loved vintage objects, and I

"I didn't need a table and chairs," says Mary Anne Thomson, "but this set was too great to pass up. It cost $100, and it made me smile—it looks like red lipstick." The kitchen set inspired Mary Anne to look for 1940s restaurant china to go with it.

①

1 Using yard sale trophies, such as vintage draperies and botanical prints, Mary Anne creates easygoing comfort in the living room. For an instant slipcover, she secured a chenille curtain panel to the sofa with safety pins. **2** Stacked books not only offer Mary Anne's guests interesting reading, but they also create a pedestal to display shells.

found everything for this house at low prices—I never spent a lot. I got things that I felt belonged in a cottage and had a cozy look."

To decorate the guest cottage, she says, "I wanted everything old, secondhand, like it had been in the family awhile." She achieves that accumulated-over-time look by mixing furniture styles freely. To make sure the results look pulled together—rather than haphazardly thrown together—she chooses pieces for their power to evoke a particular time and place. She also uses doses of red in varying amounts as a thread tying one room to the next.

Mary Anne takes the mix-not-match approach to working with vintage fabrics as well, and she finds

❶ A 1930s velvet pillow underscores the note of red that dances from room to room. **❷** Mary Anne looks for things that "sing" to her, like this vintage Panama hat and 1930s lyre-back chair, wearing its original leather upholstery.

2

that the more you have, the better. For example, she couldn't resist the richness of the red-flowered bark cloth draperies in one bedroom. She added a bark cloth comforter, quilts, and Native American blankets snapped up at a Clarksville yard sale. "The more colors I put in there, the better it got."

Red plays the keynote, however. The bright red spool cabinet on the wall emphasizes the color theme in the prints and gives the eye a place to rest. Found at a Missouri flea market, it appealed to her because it was different and quirky. Style labels are less important than the way an object looks or makes her feel. "The lines, the look of something, and how it appeals to me are what matters," she says.

color is key

Decorating the cottage lets Mary Anne indulge her passion for color and pattern. "I'll buy something because I love the colors. I may not have anything to go with it or anyplace to use it, but if it sings to me—and the price is right—I'll get it because I'll eventually find a place for it."

Native American blankets draped over the headboard create a padded effect. An occasional table stands tall enough to serve as a nightstand beside the high bed.

In the second bedroom, a carved side chair wears a gathered skirt and a tie-on apron back. Mary Anne says she bought it that way; the skirt hides a leg that was replaced. "I find a lot of things like that around here. People keep objects because they love them or because they need to, and just patch or cover up if something needs repair." She dresses the beds in a mix of new linens and vintage pillows and bedspreads. The crocheted pillows and antique spreads create the time-worn look she loves, but the sheets and coverlets are washable and easy to care for.

Most of her garage-sale purchases—furniture, draperies, rugs, and lamps—continue to serve

Refashion old draperies or use scraps of vintage fabric to slipcover a side chair. A tie-on

their original purposes. Accessories, such as old suitcases, hat boxes, and an antique sewing kit, function more as props, creating atmosphere. "I like the whole environment," says Mary Anne. "It feels like you're on vacation here. I enjoy setting the stage for guests, so when they arrive, the music is playing, and it's showtime!"

Create comfort by mixing new washable bed linens with vintage decorative pillows and coverlets. A wicker table puts a reading lamp, clock, and books in easy reach.

back shows off fancy woodwork, while the skirt can hide badly scuffed legs or a worn seat.

The hand on this metal washstand originally held a light fixture over a stairway in a turn-of-the-century house. Mary Anne rested it on the washstand for fun.

Well-worn but still usable chairs and a painted farm table turn the porch into an outdoor dining spot. The 1940s stacked lettuce-leaf bowls belonged to Mary Anne's mother and were used (appropriately enough) for serving salad.

serene & sublime

although the Seattle home of Stephen Rutledge and R. Rolfe is tiny—just 750 square feet—it feels serene. There's an air of well-worn comfort with a European pedigree, thanks to a few key antiques Rolfe acquired in Brussels in the 1970s. There's also a sense of humor—and a creative sense of style—at work, evidenced in the graphic black-and-white molding that crowns each room and in the architectural collages that frame doors and windows.

Stephen and Rolfe are inveterate junkers. "We are really attracted to decrepit objects, especially metal and wood," says Stephen. They collect architectural elements, doors, windows, finials, doorknobs, and small pieces of trimwork or molding, which Rolfe incorporates into three-dimensional assemblages or into the fabric of the house. (The constructed pediment, opposite, is an example.) "We try to make our house and garden appear as if they'd been there a long time and had fallen into a certain amount of disrepair before being rediscovered—à la *The Secret Garden*," says Stephen.

To create an overdoor pediment, R. Rolfe hung a pair of handcarved sconces on the door frame and surmounted them with a carved cornice and a triangular piece of painted and gilded wood. Printer's blocks line the lintel.

1 Shutters add visual weight to the mirror above the 19th-century Belgian sideboard. Stephen Rutledge played the bass as a child. The overdoor shelf displays a collection of oil cans. **2** Dog paintings and prints of various sizes have been hung close together and snug against the mirror to form a visual unit.

The house itself is perhaps the quintessential example of repurposing: It was originally a houseboat that was moved to dry land and converted into a mother-in-law apartment for a larger house on the same property. Stephen and Rolfe acquired it and remodeled it extensively inside, but left the shell intact. "Our house has two rooms," says Stephen. "We refer to them as 'the room' and 'the other room.'" There's also a sleeping loft and a galley-size kitchen. In the summer, the garden becomes an outdoor living room (see pages 190–93).

Textured plaster walls create the aged look they appreciate; soft colors and light woodwork enhance the tranquil feeling. Furnishings, such as the 1810 Louis Philippe sideboard and couch, anchor spaces with a quiet sophistication, and collections are organized to convey a feeling of order rather than clutter. Visitors might assume that Stephen and Rolfe's furnishings and accessories came from high-end antiques shops, but they'd be wrong. "I'm more of a garbage hound than an antiques seeker," says Stephen. "I walk everywhere and I hardly ever come home without something. One night I was walking the dogs and found an old sitz bath that had been thrown out. It's a fountain in the garden now."

"We frequent several salvage places," says Stephen, "because the merchandise changes constantly. We prefer junk stores and garage sales to antiques stores because the prices are better." Even the 19th-century antiques were flea market

❷

①

bargains acquired in the 1970s, before such pieces were widely appeciated.

"We use stuff as we find it," says Stephen, "so we tend not to restore. We like our carpets worn, we like seeing the layers of paint. That's very popular now, but we've always liked it."

If they transform something, it's likely to be an artistic enhancement rather than a restoration. They found an old garage door, for example, and set it up to define the kitchen as a separate area (see page 77). Rolfe pasted antique wallpaper over the wooden insets, then painted the wallpaper gold. "We liked the juxtaposition of the old door and the gilded paper," says Stephen.

A performer whose acting credits include *Drug Store Cowboy*, *Singles*, and *Murder She Wrote*, Stephen has been a collector since he was 15. He began with art pottery, which he still uses and displays in the kitchen. His collection of orbs—anything round, from marbles to bowling balls—inhabits the sideboard and the garden. The overdoor shelf in the dining area alternately displays old oil cans and old bug sprayers. He has begun exploring online auctions, but he says, "It's no substitute for the adventure of going out early in the morning and finding something you can't believe is available at such a low price."

① Now fitted with a mirror, this 17th-century carved panel once framed a sleeping cubicle in a Flemish working-class home.
② The shutters from the Flemish panel hang at a window in the living area.

Displayed on open
shelving, Stephen's
collection of art pottery
is both aesthetically
pleasing and functional.
Rolfe embellished the
kitchen window with
old moldings.

Rolfe pasted antique wallpaper in the panels of an old garage door, then painted them gold. He nailed half of a Gothic window frame to the door and beam, suggesting a ruined architectural support. The green-and-white cast-iron stove below it came from Brussels.

objects found

turning flea market and dustbin finds into furniture and architecture is a specialty of Ned Hand and Marcel Albanese. Both have a knack for seeing clever possibilities in old objects, and Marcel has a natural talent for making things. Their combination of abilities gave rise to a joint business venture; later, it inspired the couple to turn a rundown loft into a comfortable, contemporary apartment.

Marcel graduated with a degree in architecture in the mid-1980s, but with the scarcity of jobs, he turned to product design. He also began creating what he called "refurniture," reusing objects initially built for some other purpose. Ned came to this country from Ireland after graduating from high school. She met Marcel, and together with a partner, they founded Studio F.KIA. Marcel and the partner designed and manufactured gift and bath products and produced his refurniture, while Ned handled the retail end of the business.

Now Ned runs her own home furnishings store, called Fresh Eggs ("everything for your nest"). Marcel does custom interior work, designing, building, and

Windows salvaged from an old office building have been joined with screws to make a see-through wall dividing the living area from the bedroom in this Boston loft.

Streamlined shapes link old
and new pieces in the living
area. In this setting, old
photographer's lights look
right at home as floor lamps.
The leaded-glass window,
which came from an antiques
shop, screens the view of the
building next door.

Check salvage yards or sites of commercial renovations for discarded wood-frame windows.

installing room partitions, credenzas, islands, and other furnishings built from industrial materials. "Marcel can do anything," says Ned, and the couple's loft proves that she's right. Working with basic supplies from a home improvement center and the found objects he and Ned collect, Marcel turned the cavernous loft into spacious but functional areas for cooking, dining, relaxing, and sleeping.

carving out space

To separate the living area from the bedroom, they created a see-through wall of windows

They can be the starting point for cabinets, room dividers, tabletops, and picture frames.

gathered from an old office building that was being renovated. Ned says, "We wanted the bedroom to be separate, but we still wanted the space to flow." A sisal rug anchors the furniture grouping in the living area; the natural texture and neutral color make a simple, unfussy ground for modern furniture. The Italian couch is new, from Ned's shop, but the rest of the furnishings are largely thrift-shop finds and Marcel's creative adaptations. "We have an eye for seeing [the possibilities] in something that's not much," says Marcel. "We're pretty lighthearted about it, but when we see

1 Long drywall screws attach the bowling pins to the bottom of a metal World War II case for gas masks. The case now stores photos. The couple fills the gumball machines on top with different items according to the occasion: candy corn for Halloween parties, aspirin for Christmas, and mints for other gatherings. **2** Ned and Marcel collected "lost" drawers, then Marcel built individual boxes from ¾-inch plywood to house each one. The drawers store odds and ends.

1 An old hospital gurney becomes a dining table with the addition of a plywood top. The chandelier was made from stock goosenecks from an electrical supply company. **2** They began their collection of oil cans by accident: Marcel bought a box of them at a flea market and became fascinated by the different sizes, shapes, and types.

something that appeals to us, we say, 'What else could it be? What else could it do?'"

decorating for fun

Out of that lighthearted approach come whimsical pieces that take visitors by surprise—and make them laugh. A table with bowling-pin legs, gumball machines as sculpture, and a chandelier that resembles an octopus with multicolored feet all attest to this couple's slightly wacky take on home furnishings.

   In the dining area, white paint covers walls, ceilings, pipes, and an original ventilation unit, blending them into the background without denying the loft's frankly industrial roots. New modern chairs draw up to a table made from a hospital gurney. The couple acquired it from a woodworking shop, where it was being used to move large items. They mounted plywood to the gurney from underneath and edged the top with a solid maple 1×3-inch strip for a finished look. Marcel also designed the chandelier, using stock goosenecks (for desk lamps) from an electrical supply company. Sold through F.KIA, the fixture has a dome made of spun aluminum, but Marcel suggests that a restaurant-size colander could be used to achieve a similar effect.

   For storage, Marcel turned a collection of mismatched drawers—from sewing cabinets, dressers, and desks—into a stacking cabinet. He built a plywood box to contain each drawer and attached wheels to the bottom box so the cabinet can be moved as a unit. The drawers store tools, supplies, and found objects awaiting new uses. "If I'm working on a project, I can take the whole box to the table with

me and keep everything together," he says. Ned adds, "We are always looking for found objects, and there is always a new project to work on. When we need something, we like to make it or find it, if possible."

handcrafted kitchen

To define the kitchen and make it the focal point of the living area, they raised it on a platform. The lower cabinets were built on site from plywood and medium-density fiberboard. A break in the cabinets at the sink end lets visitors enter the kitchen by stepping up onto the platform. A polyurethane finish protects the wood and emphasizes its natural golden color.

For the upper cabinets, the couple started with salvaged windows and built boxes to fit them. To provide good work lights over the countertops, they simply dropped electrical cable from the ceiling, added sockets, and covered the bulbs with tin shades bought at a flea market for $1 each. They collected '50s dishes at flea markets too. The bar stools are old school chairs; Marcel extended the legs by pushing ¾-inch electrical conduit inside the hollow chair legs. The glides from the original chair feet just popped onto the end of the conduit to finish off the legs.

Custom-built cabinets on a platform define the kitchen area, and modified school chairs draw up to the counter. To make the wall cabinets, Marcel started with salvaged windows and built boxes to fit.

①

creative storage

In the bedroom, instead of using the usual chest of drawers for storage, Ned keeps her out-of-season clothes in a pyramid of old suitcases, which the couple has been collecting for years. Other clothes tuck away neatly in the drawers Marcel created from a baker's rack and plywood (see the photo opposite). "We found the baker's rack in the trash," says Marcel. "I knew immediately what I wanted to do with it." He made the drawers from a single 4×8-foot sheet of ½-inch ash plywood, designing them to fit snugly between the shelves of the baker's rack. For the drawer pulls, he used a ¼-inch tap-and-die kit from a hardware store to make threaded holes in printer's type. Then he used a machine screw to attach the type to the drawer from inside.

For this couple, shopping garage sales and flea markets is a means to an end; they're motivated by the desire for thrifty, unusual items with which to furnish their home rather than by a passion for collecting. "If something excites us, we think about it and then we might get it," says Marcel. "We don't really 'consume' a lot." If faced with a choice between buying something new and something old, however, they'll opt for the secondhand. "A lot of old stuff still works, so we usually buy something that's older and fix it up."

2

1 A 1950s gooseneck desk lamp throws light onto the ceiling for an ambient glow. **2** The narrow chest of drawers was a baker's rack rescued from the trash; Marcel built the drawers from ash plywood. He also constructed the bed, using stock lumber from a home improvement center. The chair was another streetside find, which Marcel's sister revived with new yellow suede upholstery.

fifties plus

terri and Dale Anderson don't consider themselves devotees of modernism as such. "We are drawn to objects of interesting design," says Terri. "Age is less important. So our loft combines things from the 1800s to the 1980s. A piece may intrigue us because of its form, texture, or history."

The chain hanging from the ceiling in the living area, for example, is Amish, made from bottle caps strung together on wire and fastened into loops to serve as fencing. Lined up on the half-wall that separates the bedroom from the living area, wooden exercise pins reflect attitudes toward health and fitness at the turn of the century: Exercise as a means to good health was a new idea, and these pins, carved by cabinetmakers during their offseason, were used as weights to strengthen muscles.

Combined with these vintage objects are pristine examples of 20th-century design. Sculptor Isamu Noguchi, a major figure in the mid-20th-century modernist movement, designed the pair of light sculptures, crouching like friendly aliens on

Parachutes from an army surplus store cover the windows with a white-on-white spider web pattern in this Boston loft. Modern art mixes with antiques and flea market finds: Paper light sculptures flank a 19th-century trunk topped with kilim pillows.

1 Stacked suitcases do double duty as a side table and storage for winter clothes. Made of resin-coated woven cane over a plywood base, they were made by OshKosh, a top-of-the-line manufacturer in the 1930s and 1940s. **2** Although not flea market finds, these carved wooden figures by Mexican artist Hippolito have an abstract quality that suits the spirit of modern furniture. **3** The chain, made from bottle caps strung together on wire and fastened into loops, once fenced an Amish farm.

each side of a 19th-century trunk. The molded plywood and tubular-steel chairs around the dining table are icons of mid-1950s furniture. The table itself was designed in the 1930s, the inventive work of Swedish designer Bruno Mathsson; it collapses to 12 inches in length and expands to 12 feet. The 1950s Heywood-Wakefield dresser, desk, and chair in the bedroom are highly prized pieces from America's premier manufacturer of modern furniture for the masses.

unified with white

To tie these different pieces together, the couple painted the loft's walls, floors, and ceilings sparkling white and draped filmy white parachutes over the windows. The result is a luminous setting that emphasizes the sculptural quality of each object. The neutral palette of black leather upholstery, golden wood, and natural sisal underscores the fresh, clean effect.

Terri and Dale like to mix ethnic and American folk art with their modern pieces. "They bring a necessary warmth," says Terri. "They have an innocence and charm that work well with modern furniture."

The couple also introduces character with repurposed flea market finds. "Our passion has become the use or reuse of elements for purposes for which they were not intended," says Terri. "Most of the time we know what an object could become, but other times it evolves." They knew immediately when they found the pipe-organ section (now sitting on the dining table) that they would fill it with candles of graduated heights as a pun on its original purpose. Dale cut dowels to the required heights and rested votive candles on the dowels.

2

3

modern revival

Modernism, which began in the 1920s, embraced new technology and industrial materials such as tubular steel, molded plywood, and plastic. Furniture design was to be rational and functional, with no reference to historical styles. The furniture didn't catch on in America until after World War II and fell from favor by 1960.

Throughout the 1970s, however, classics such as Mies van der Rohe's Barcelona chair or Marcel Breuer's Wassily chair continued to define the spirit of the age. By the 1980s, collectors were beginning to snap up pieces from the 1940s and 1950s. Yet, Terri maintains, even their most valuable pieces were flea market prizes found in the mid-1990s. "The Bruno Mathsson table was purchased at a flea market for $150. Our desk is the most collected piece of all Heywood-Wakefield furniture. We found it in Texas and paid $300 for it."

rising prices

"In the last three to five years, modern furniture has skyrocketed," she continues. "It's harder to find, but if you look, you still can find good investment pieces." Some of the best places to search are in the Midwest and South. Because

The furniture grouping centers on the sofa and a coffee table-on-wheels, designed by Terri and built by Dale. A sisal rug helps define the living area. The red bowl was a 1940s promotional record album that Dale put in the oven until it melted; then he shaped it to recall the free-form designs of '50s vases.

To combine modern and antique pieces in fresh, uncluttered rooms, look for harmonies of line and shape. The severe geometry of a 1930s table echoes that of a 19th-century American trunk, while the curves of 1950s chairs repeat the outlines of a 19th-century Turkish olive jar and a rhinoceros skin shield from Nigeria.

When Dale and Terri spotted this section of a 19th-century pipe organ, they knew right away that they wanted to fill the pipes with candles.

An early-19th-century blacksmith's bellows hangs like art above the bed, while a new aluminum tool chest for pickup trucks provides end-of-bed storage for blankets and clothes. On the trunk sits a coal thrasher: It was originally used to break up coal stuck in factory chutes. "It's utilitarian," says Dale, "but it is also a cool object."

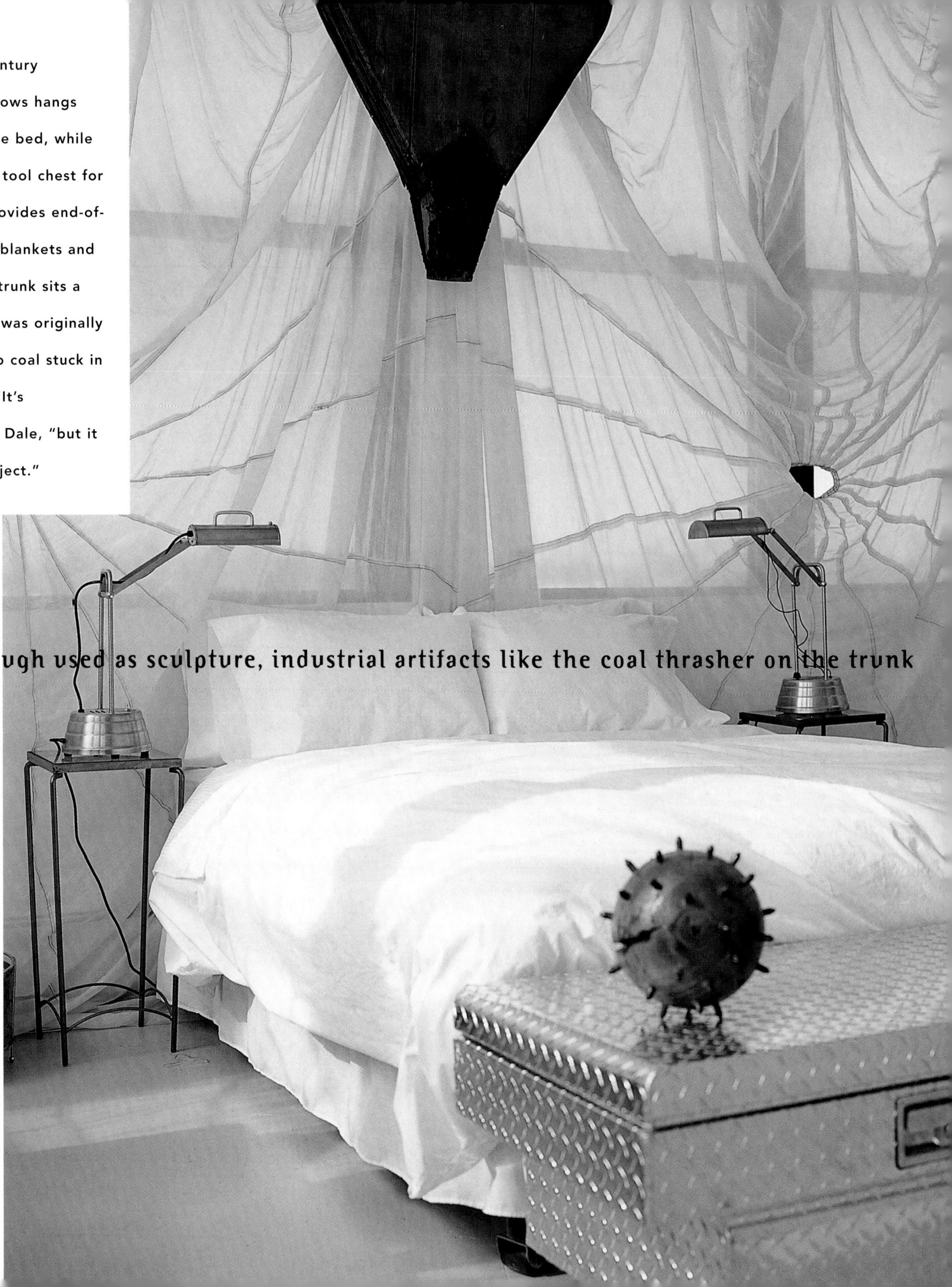

Although used as sculpture, industrial artifacts like the coal thrasher on the trunk

modern furniture is highly valued in New York and Los Angeles, prices are higher there, says Terri. "We're still in the midst of furniture changing hands from the first generation to the second here in Boston," she adds. "Prices start going up when the third generation starts buying."

do your homework

The problem with evaluating prices for modern furniture is that a piece may have been designed in the 1950s, but it still may be manufactured today. To determine whether a molded-plywood Eames chair is old or new, for example, you need

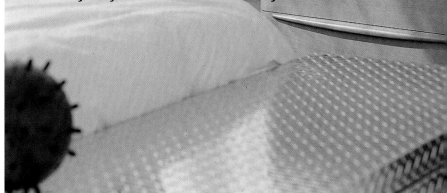

or the bellows above the bed are more interesting if you know their original functions.

to know that the chair was originally produced only in certain finishes. Condition is also critical.

Knowing the labels to look for and the provenance—who has owned it and for how long—also will help you identify a piece. Terri cautions, however, that there are still many unknowns in the field of modern furniture.

for love and money

Terri was retail director for the Museum of Fine Arts, Houston, for 12 years, and Dale built custom-designed furniture. Both are longtime collectors; now they've put that passion to work, selling new and collectible furniture and accessories at their store, Abodeon, in Cambridge, Massachusetts. Every week, they head out to

To enjoy furnishings and accessories for their sculptural qualities, eliminate distracting clutter and edit displays to a few of your best or favorite things.

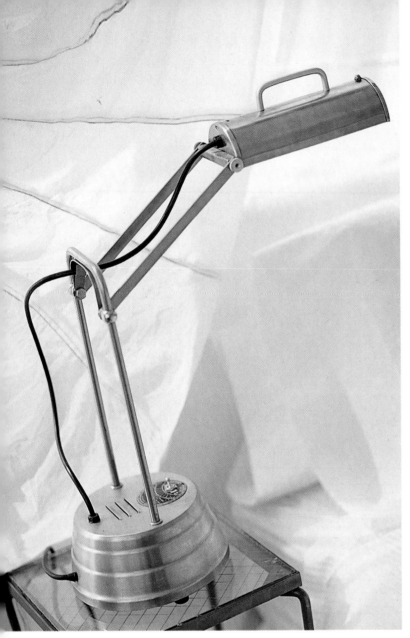

flea markets. "Sometimes we just wander," says Dale. "We always come back with something."

These days, their finds usually end up at the shop rather than at home. "We've been creating all of our lives but no longer feel the need to have a lot of possessions," explains Terri. "There are a few things that are sacred to us, but for the most part, they're only objects. The thrill is in the chase, never knowing what you'll find. The acquisition can be gratifying, but the real pleasure is often the search."

dale and terri's advice

"Buy what you like, buy what you can afford, and buy the best you can afford."

"Look for quality. The more you look, the better your eye will be. Go to galleries, museums, stores, flea markets. Do a lot of research before you buy, and talk to dealers to find out what they know."

"Don't buy something just because it's inexpensive. We've all done that, and you end up with something you don't need. It may cost only $5, but if you don't love it, what's the point?"

To learn more about modernism, check out *1000 Chairs* by Charlotte and Peter Fiell (Taschen, 1997), *Mid-Century Modern* by Cara Greenberg (Harmony Books, 1984, 1995), and *Heywood-Wakefield Modern Furniture* by Steve and Roger Rouland (Collector Books, 1995, 1997).

A steel-and-glass night table made by a Texas artist holds a 1920s tanning lamp that was originally used for health treatments.

The Heywood-Wakefield desk and chair represent mid-century modernism for the masses. The molded-plywood chair with tubular-steel legs, designed by Danish architect Arne Jacobsen, has been in production ever since it was introduced in 1955.

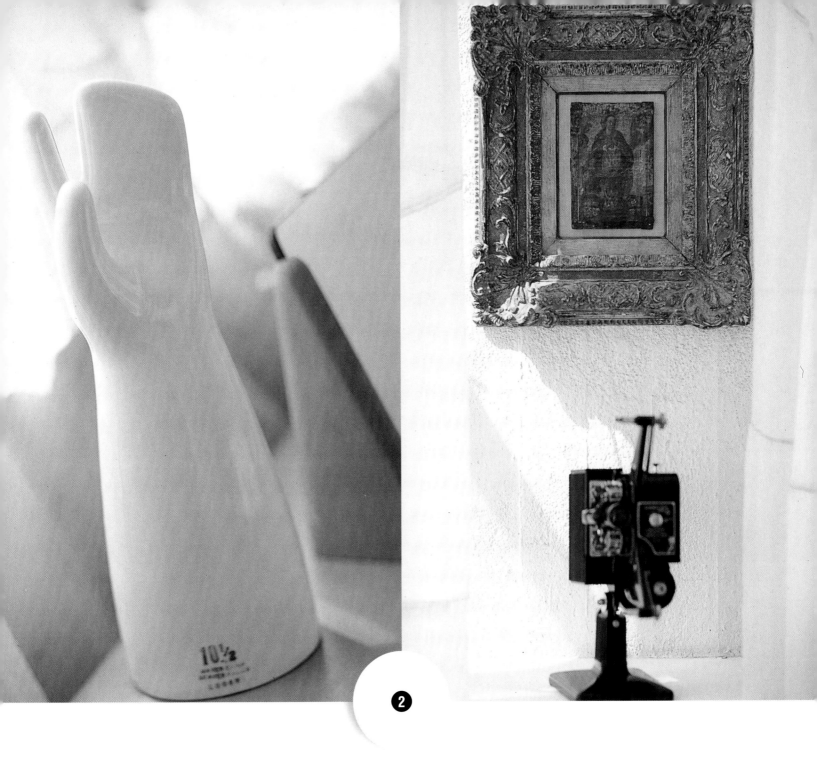

2

1 A collection of wooden exercise pins is unified by warm wood tones. You could create a similar effect with glass bottles, pottery vases, or porch spindles in a single color. **2** A pristine white background shows to advantage a glove form, rare for its undivided fingers; an 18th-century Mexican religious painting; and a 1930s film projector, appreciated for its form.

modern country

amela Fritz brings French country style to San Francisco—
but it's not the French Country of the 1980s, when Pierre Dieux
and saturated Mediterranean hues were the rage. "It's a more
natural approach, with hemp and cotton sheets on daybeds so
it's more comfy and homey" she explains. "It's wrinkled and
rumpled and casual." Hues are light and clean, with strong jolts of color
used sparingly as accents. Old metal furniture and accessories keep the
look airy, linear, and fresh.

"I like things to be very comfortable," says Pamela. "Everything is rustic, but the
approach is modern—I use natural fabrics, and everything is scaled down and
scaled back, with light colors and no clutter. Everything looks lived in."

Flea market finds, especially French ones, are an essential ingredient in Pamela's
approach to decorating. They provide vintage character and a look of age, giving
rooms a feeling of being connected to a romantic, storied past. She prefers rusted
or painted metal garden furniture because its clean, graceful lines enhance the

With Pamela Fritz's no-fuss
approach to decorating, you
simply can wrap the worn
seats of French club chairs
with fabric instead of
reupholstering them.

Generous amounts of white, combined with rustic and rusted-metal textures, are key to the modern country look. Playing off a hue in the hanging sap cans, the heavy velvet draperies add color without disturbing the serenity of the room.

breezy look of her interiors. Metal accessories such as zinc water pitchers, wire baskets, and metal storage crates are vintage, but they introduce a contemporary note because they bring to mind industrial materials.

french flea

"I'm a flea market queen," says Pamela. "My mom was like that. I remember her taking us to the Salvation Army store, only she called it 'Sally's,' so I thought it was the name of a department store! We went to garage sales and auctions all the time too."

Now Pamela and her business partners, Fred and Coco Testu, travel to France six times a year to shop flea markets and to scour the countryside for pieces to sell in their wholesale shop, Intérieur Perdu (Lost Interior). The Testus grew up on a horse farm in the Loire Valley, where their parents still live, so their childhood home provides a convenient place to store purchases. One of the trio's favorite shopping spots is L'isle sur La Sorgue, a town that periodically turns into one huge flea market. "It's not cheap," says Pamela, "but you can get some good deals. We shop with the spiders and dirt and really dig to find things. Not everyone likes to shop that way."

1 A late 19th-century clock face from Normandy hangs at one end of the living room. On the workbench below, a zinc water pitcher, a pair of 1930s red bowls, and a French food safe form an uncluttered display. Although the rules usually dictate using uneven numbers of objects, one red bowl wouldn't have had enough visual weight, so the pair acts as one. **2** Sap cans in assorted sizes and colors hang on nails, creating a three-dimensional painting.

1 A birdbath on a tall, graceful pedestal functions as indoor sculpture. Pamela usually places a shallow bowl of gardenias in it. **2** The scalloped-edge containers on the table are French funeral vases; Pamela fills them with moss or apples or uses them as trays.

1

new country style

Pamela's contemporary country style starts with a light, clear palette of color. White walls, ceilings, and floors create a clean, blank-canvas backdrop for furnishings and accessories in the living room and guest room. In the bedroom, soft yellow-green walls inject color while preserving the feeling of tranquility.

Instead of crowding rooms with fussy fabrics and dense collections of objects and furnishings, Pamela keeps things simple. For easy-care slipcovers, she tosses hemp sheets over the sofa and chairs. When she needs extra seating, she pulls in vintage bistro chairs.

Instead of paintings or prints, Pamela hangs colorful sap cans on the wall like a three-dimensional painting (see page 109). "For parties, I fill them with candles. It's beautiful at night," she says. "Or I'll put juice glasses in them to hold water and put a single flower in each can."

Displays are carefully edited to allow her favorite objects to show well. Most have stories attached. The clock face on page 108 came from a 19th-century church in Normandy; the 1930s red bowls on the table below came from her hometown in Iowa; and a green French food safe, which dates to the 1930s or 1940s, would have been hung from a tree to keep food beyond the reach of animals. Under the table, old French army boxes now hold magazines.

rust in peace

Because Pamela likes the look of rusted surfaces, she doesn't remove the corrosion from metal furniture she finds. "We clean things up and repair them, but we don't restore," she says. Instead, she brushes the object vigorously with a wire brush, then rubs it with boiled linseed oil from the hardware store. "Linseed oil is magic stuff," she says. "It rehydrates metal and punches up the color." She lets the linseed oil soak in overnight, then wipes off the excess. If you want to prevent any further flaking, she recommends spraying the piece with a clear matte finish.

Pamela uses linseed oil on old painted furniture, too, to intensify the color. A coat of paste wax

1 A zinc water pitcher holds green calla lilies in the living room, hinting at the color to come in the bedroom. **2** Pamela found the old door with the mirror already installed in it. Leaning against the wall, it serves as a full-length dressing mirror. Old gas station numbers hang on the wall for whimsy and a lively jolt of color.

provides a durable finish. "Paste wax also reconditions dry leather," she adds, but if the leather is so dehydrated that it's crumbly, then it's beyond salvaging.

Pamela grew up on a farm in Burlington, Iowa. Gifted with both creativity and an entrepreneurial spirit, she skipped college and went to work in visual merchandising at Marshall Field's in Dallas. ("I was a window dresser, though now they're called stylists," she says.) A job as visual director for I. Magnin brought her to San Francisco. "It was a wonderful training ground, but I wanted to

Metal garden furniture helps create a light, airy feeling in the bedroom. On the tables, French apothecary measuring jars hold flowers. If you find only one pair of antique swing-arm drapery rods, use them on the center window for emphasis, as Pamela did in the bay window.

"I like to lean mirrors against the wall instead of hanging them," says Pamela. "It softens

work for myself," she says. She designed and manufactured miniature wire chairs and other metal objects before teaming up with the Testus, who share her decorating aesthetic.

"I don't like things to match," says Pamela. "I mix all the decades and centuries. That's what's fun about flea market decorating—it's very personal and very inspiring, and it looks like it has been collected over time. No one can exactly duplicate the look you create for yourself. I like that."

things so they don't look so perfect. I don't like things to match."

1 In the guest bedroom, a turn-of-the-century American cast-iron bed and French garden furniture wear coats of rust. The bulbous glass jar is a French *damejane* (pronounced dom-jon), originally used to hold homemade wine. **2** In the bathroom, a swivel office chair adjusts to a comfortable height for applying makeup. In the 1920s medical cabinet, antique liquid measuring jars from a French apothecary hold makeup brushes.

1

bringing it home

Hunting for objects with character is half the fun; finding a home for each of your new treasures is the other half. The following pages offer dozens of ideas for using flea market finds in every room in the house. Look for similar items when you shop, or let the ideas inspire you to discover creative new uses for objects you already have.

livingrooms

What better place to put your treasures to work (and express your personality) than in the living room or den where you relax with family and friends?

Look to secondhand stores, flea markets, and thrift shops to find handy tables for books and drinks, storage for music and television, seating pieces, and elements to create a focal point. Then layer on character and charm with accessories, art, and collectibles.

Anything with a flat top can serve as a coffee table or side table. Trunks, chests, boxes, and lidded wicker baskets offer the added value of extra storage space. Any item that can support a sheet of glass can become a table, too. For the best buy, check import stores for precut glass tabletops. If you can't find the size you need, have a glass company cut a piece for you. Use ⅜- to ½-inch-thick glass and have the edges seamed to eliminate sharpness; for a more attractive finish (and a small additional fee), you can ask the glass company to polish the whole width of each edge so it's flat and smooth.

Set the stage for comfort with a plump sofa and club chair, and draw up wicker chairs, an old rocker, and even old office furniture to fill out the conversational cluster. If you prefer the look of vintage upholstered chairs and sofas, shop for

Comfortable overscaled sofas
pull up to a large wicker basket
that serves as a coffee table.
Let an interesting old picture
frame make its own statement:
Hang it on the chimney breast,
and prop one or two lightweight
items inside it.

1

2

pieces with good lines and sturdy construction;
reupholstery can be expensive, however, so be
sure the piece is worth it (see pages 198–201
for tips on evaluating furniture).

Use the room's natural focal point (usually a
fireplace) to make a style statement by
displaying your favorite things there. Or use an
armoire or cupboard as a stage for showing off
objects that appeal to you.

1 New velvet and damask pillows and cushions gave
this Edwardian sofa a fresh lease on life. **2** Keep an
eye out for vintage buttons, tassels, and trims to add an
elegant touch to pillows stitched from rich fabrics.

1 A corroded oil drum picks up the metallic texture of worn gilding on French chairs. Found in a dump, it was cut down to about 4 inches above the height of the seats and topped by a 30-inch round of glass. **2** Turn a wall-mount kitchen cabinet on its side to serve as a table and bookcase. The shelves hold your favorite books upright. Be aware that paint manufactured before 1978 probably contains lead, so if you have children who are teething (and likely to chew on the wood), keep such pieces out of reach. (See page 204 for more information.)

②

❶ Simple feet cut from 1x4-inch lumber raise an old drum to end-table height. At chairside, a petite doll's dresser displays books and collectibles. For quick slipcovers on thrift-shop wicker, simply wrap bark cloth or vintage tablecloths around cushions, pinning the fabric underneath. **❷** A child's picnic table and bench, discovered at the Pasadena Rose Bowl Flea Market, sidles up to a sofa to hold books or drinks. Homeowner Beth Ruggiero matted and framed the Chanel advertisement, using a wide mat to give it the importance of a print.

To enhance a space with gentle light, take a tip from designer Jean Alan: Trim old mirrors and glue them in a grid to plywood. Use Mirror Mastic to attach the mirrors; other adhesives could ruin the silver.

how to make a decorative finial:

Turn a set of ball-and-claw feet, perhaps from a table or a piano stool, into finials for a curtain rod, using a dowel and screws. The metal leg already has a hole in it. You can find dowels at crafts stores and hardware stores. Check with a hardware store for the right size roundhead screw to fit the hole.

1 Use No. 0000 steel wool and mineral spirits (or vinegar and water) to scrub off any rust and grime from the metal. Apply a coat of paste wax to protect the cleaned metal.

2 Buy a dowel to fit the top of the metal leg (this one was ¾ inch). Paint the dowel the desired color, then mark the position for the screw.

3 Drill a starter hole for the screw to keep the wood from splitting. Position the metal leg over the dowel and insert the screw.

4 To hold the drapery rod in place, screw a painted-metal or brass mug hook into the window frame on each side of the window. (Mug hooks are wide enough to receive a ¾-inch dowel. Look for them in chain discount stores or hardware stores.)

1 If you have one commanding piece, like this leaded-glass window from France, let it dominate your mantel display. For visual balance, frame it with tall, weighty architectural elements or candlesticks (these were made from balusters and salvaged wood). Ordinary candlesticks would look wimpy here, too small for the window. **2** To screen a fireplace when it's not in use, carefully fold a section of pressed-tin ceiling panel so it stands upright. Propping a rusted metal tractor seat against it, overlapping the edge of the fireplace, ties the fire screen visually to the architecture.

❶ Decorating problem: a poorly placed air-conditioner that's an eyesore. Creative solution: shop the flea market for a picture frame the same size or a little larger than the unit (cost: about $20). Paint it a neutral color, have a mirror cut to fit the opening, and during the months when you don't need the air-conditioner, hang the framed mirror over the unit. ❷ A decorative knob mounted on the wall above the air-conditioner and a swag of fabric provide a finishing flourish.

❶

2

1 You can angle the top of this lap table for writing, but here it's used as a miniature table to create levels for an artful display.
2 Showcase a photo by framing it with architecture. Instead of centering the photo inside the round window frame, position it closer to the bottom so it feels anchored.

2

❶ Although you could display interesting old outdoor faucet handles as art objects on a wall or in a bowl, why not put them to work holding pillar candles? ❷ Washington, D.C., artist Rick Singleton bought seven 1940s rearview mirrors at a basement sale for $7. Most already had holes for screws so he just mounted them on the wall. For those without holes, he cut a wooden template that he screwed to the wall, then attached the mirror base to the template. The mirrors make excellent sconces for votive candles.

2

1 Use a neutral color scheme for walls, furniture, and art to knit objects together and create a clean, serene look. Turn a mannequin head into whimsical sculpture by giving her a stack of straw hats to wear. The folding stool was an old redwood patio stool with a torn canvas seat; it was easily revived by sanding off some of the stain to let the wood grain show and replacing the canvas with fabric tacked in place.

2 Look for trophy cups or loving cups to hold cutlery, napkins, or flowers. Victorian comb holders can round up sewing notions or mail.

❶ A child's red wagon can hold mail, magazines, or office supplies. At 10x12 inches, it's a good size to rest on the floor or on a square coffee table. **❷** A toy wagon makes an unexpected candy dish. Before putting food in a toy like this, be sure to wash the toy in hot, soapy water; line it with plastic if you like. Old milk bottles readily serve as flower vases, but if you're a serious collector, you'll probably want to keep the real gems of your collection safely locked away. Depending on the logos, dairy of origin, and rarity, they can cost $50 to $100.

3 Look for sections of iron fencing to hang up as coat racks. In an entry, this decorative garden fence takes up little space and is just the right size for children's jackets. **4** Always ask yourself "What else can this be?" A ship's ladder from an old freighter has steps the right width to display a collection of boats gathered from various flea markets.

diningrooms

Use flea market finds and garage sale treasures to furnish your dining area. Start with the basics—table and chairs—or launch your scheme with an antique storage piece that you love.

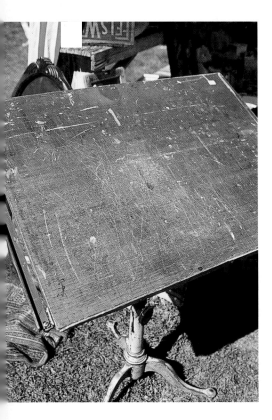

When you're shopping for dining room furniture, it's particularly important to have the measurements of your room handy and to carry a small tape measure. In addition to measuring the table to see if it will fit, remember to add 24 to 36 inches on each side to allow room for chairs to be pulled out comfortably. Keep in mind the shape of your room, too. A square dining area calls for a square or round table, while a rectangular room can accommodate either a rectangular or an oval one.

While it's possible to find dining room tables with matching chairs at flea markets, it's more fun to mix and match—and you may be able to furnish the room more economically than if you buy a complete suite of furniture. Mixing and matching works whether your style is formal or casual. For a comfortable, country feeling, choose a sturdy farmhouse table and collect a variety of painted chairs to pull up around it. To guarantee visual harmony, vary the shapes but keep the colors similar. If you like to shake things up a bit, vary both the styles and the colors, but make

"Vary and repeat" is the theme song for creating harmonious room designs. Bring a variety of chairs to the table for a casual, "collected over time" look, but repeat the colors to create rhythm. Let one or two colors dominate (yellow and green here), and cast other colors in supporting roles.

sure the colors repeat throughout the room. In the room on page 143, for example, the worn seat and spindles of the blue chair reveal a bit of green that relates to the adjacent green-painted chair and the cupboard against the wall. Hints of blue and red on the green chair relate to both the red and the blue chairs. Repeating colors ties the room together and keeps a multi-hued palette from looking chaotic.

For a clean, contemporary feeling, paint walls white and choose bleached or golden blond wood for chairs and accents. If you haven't found the table of your dreams yet, nail a sheet of plywood to a pair of sawhorses and cover the construction with a floor-length skirt made from canvas or a painter's drop cloth.

If you prefer a more formal dining room, look for polished mahogany, walnut, cherry, or maple pieces (referred to as "brown furniture" by antiques dealers). The table's wood need not match that of the chairs—in the dining area on page 150, dark-stained Queen Anne-style chairs

---

In close quarters, use small-scale seating like these ballroom chairs. Old movie stills, purchased for $1 each, look like fine art when identically matted and framed. To give each photo more importance, make the mat as wide all around as the photo's width.

draw up to a table with a lighter color. Mahogany blends with oak in the dining room on page 151, thanks to warm reddish undertones in the stains used on both woods.

When you're shopping for chairs, don't limit yourself to those intended for the dining room. Upholstered side chairs usually destined for the living room can encourage guests to linger around the table. Look for seats that are at a comfortable height in relation to the table (18 inches from floor to seat is standard). Chairs should be easy to pull in and out, like the antique French opera chairs shown here; they're designed for comfort, yet are movable.

To enhance the mood you want to create, consider what you put underfoot and overhead. Sisal has a contemporary look that links formal and casual furnishings into a unified whole; Oriental carpets set a more formal tone. Whether you use a single rug or layer several, make sure the floor covering extends far enough to accommodate both the table and chairs.

Keep an eye out for unusual lighting fixtures at flea markets. The brass chandeliers shown on page 150 probably hung in a church originally. Instead of wiring them for electricity, the owner continues to use candles, reinforcing the romantic, exotic look of layered Oriental carpets under the table and chairs.

❶ Give your dining room a focal point by framing a view with shutters, simply leaning them against the wall. ❷ Dare to rummage: The homeowner found the lamp at the bottom of a junk pile and paid $20 for it. Topped with a new shade, it could sell for $600.

1 Turn a 1940s kitchen cart into a bar. **2** For a matte metal look, have a restorer dip your 1930s dinette set in stripper to remove old, chipped paint. Stainless steel medical containers from the 1950s can hold sugar, tea bags, or candy. A 1930s punch bowl shaped like Saturn (the cups sit on the ring) will provoke smiles and conversation.

1 Carpet the dining room with layers of small rugs instead of one large one. Let one color dominate to achieve a coherent look. **2** Don't be afraid to pair the rustic with the refined: Lacy iron grillwork and tin architectural finials serve as artwork in a room furnished with oak and mahogany.

❶ Use vintage bark cloth draperies to slipcover parsons chairs. To get the most impact from a limited amount of fabric, use the bark cloth on the chair back and make the seat, skirt, and piping from solid coordinating fabrics.

❷ If a teapot is missing its lid, use it as a flower container.

1 Fill a child's pedal-powered car with potted plants to display as a large-scale centerpiece on a banquet-size table or on the floor as a planter. **2** Use a terra-cotta chimney pot as a striking pedestal indoors or out. **3** Bring a bit of lawn indoors with wheat grass in an old berry basket. Line the wooden basket with foil before inserting a mat of wheat grass from a florist's shop. Or sow wheat berries (from a natural-foods shop) in soil in a plastic flat and then transfer the grass to the foil-lined basket.

kitchens

Beyond the dinnerware and serving pieces you may collect, bring flea market character to the kitchen with unusual storage pieces, work surfaces, and even cabinetry created from architectural salvage.

garage sales, flea markets, and thrift shops offer great deals in dishes, utensils, and even pots and pans that have vintage character but are still usable. Beware of buying secondhand appliances that you can't test first, however, and carefully check the wiring on any electrical appliances.

Storage pieces, such as painted or stripped-pine cupboards and hutches, bring warmth and character to a modern kitchen, as do work surfaces like butcher blocks or pine tables. They're functional, yet because they're pieces of furniture rather than built-ins, they relax the space and give it personality.

If you're starting from scratch, either remodeling your kitchen or building a new one, you can layer on a collected look by incorporating antiques and salvaged architecture. When Peg Shulha, a Chicago-area interior designer, turned a century-old barn into her home, she designed the kitchen with antique pine pieces in mind (see page 158). An Irish food cupboard and a massive butcher's table came from a

On a shelf made from recycled brackets and wood, French gnat catchers still serve their original purpose, attracting pesky flies and mosquitoes with sugar water. Vintage linens inspired the new kitchen towels.

local antiques store; a wall-hung pine cupboard came from the flea market in Sandwich, Illinois. For the island and the custom-built cabinets over the wall-mounted ovens, Peg used salvaged barn lumber. To lighten the effect of so much brown wood, she left the center panels of the island's drawers and cupboard doors unplaned. The refrigerator, a model with a blank door panel, also features unplaned barn siding.

Although Peg's kitchen is lofty and large-scaled, the idea of incorporating freestanding furniture and salvaged work surfaces into a new kitchen can apply to more modest homes as well. To make sure everything will fit, work with an architect or builder to determine the amount of space appliances will require. Also note where plumbing, gas, and electrical hookups need to be placed. Then measure carefully how much room you'll have available for salvaged cabinets, cupboards, pie safes, and tables—and have fun shopping!

An antique Irish food cupboard (far left) holds dinnerware, and the adjacent butcher's table provides both storage and expansive work space. Using movable furniture instead of, or in addition to, built-ins gives a kitchen warmth and flexibility.

1 You needn't confine chests of drawers to the bedroom. This pine chest stores table linens and kitchen supplies. **2** If you're remodeling your kitchen, take a tip from interior designer Peg Shulha and collect vintage wood and moldings to add character to the new construction. She found the fluted pilasters, still wearing their original blue paint, at a flea market and used them to cover the angled corners of the cabinetry framing the farm-style sink.

2

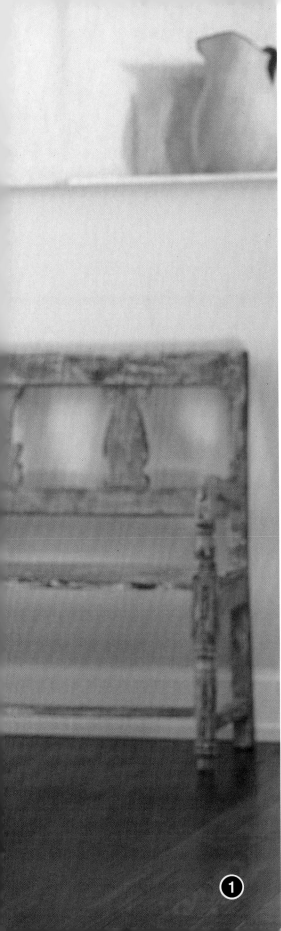

❶ Artist Floyd Gumpf's hallmark in furniture design is using reclaimed moldings with their original paint. Here they've been assembled to form a sink apron and cabinet doors. ❷ Doors constructed from old pine conceal a small refrigerator, an icemaker, and a wine cooler. Tin inserts, rescued from a dilapidated pie safe, decorate the doors. The copper bar sink came from an antiques fair.

2 A corn planter in its original red paint works well as a vase for flowers.

3 Keys remain handy with an action-figure "caddy."

1 A section of flower-bed fencing holds towels and kitchen utensils, while cast-iron bathtub feet (standing upside down) make unusual bookends. **2** A corn planter in its original red paint works well as a vase for flowers. **3** Keys remain handy with an action-figure "caddy." Artist Rick Singleton used a handheld high-speed rotary tool to grind two keyhole-shaped holes in the doll's back; then he inserted two screws into the wall the appropriate distance apart, leaving the heads protruding far enough to push the doll onto them.

1 A cobbler's cast-iron nail sorter turns on its pedestal base just like a lazy Susan. To adapt it for serving spices or condiments, wash it in soapy water, dry it well, then rub with a thin coat of vegetable oil to protect it from rusting. **2** An oil-cloth-covered tool chest from the turn of the century converts to countertop storage for flatware and linens. The chest also could hold mail, coupons, stamps, and pens or pencils. Placed on a table in a corner of the kitchen, it could serve as a mini-office for paying bills and making grocery lists.

bedrooms
& baths

From beds and bedding to storage and accessories, antiques fairs offer everything you need to furnish the bedroom of your dreams. Creative ideas for clutter control can give your bathroom character, too.

i f you long to snuggle into an antique bed, be sure to take your room measurements, including ceiling height, when you go shopping. A 9-foot-tall Renaissance Revival headboard may look grand outdoors or in an antiques warehouse but will overpower a room with 10-foot ceilings. Also be sure to measure your mattress. Antique beds (other than daybeds and single beds) range in width from 51 to 59 inches and in length from 74 to 84 inches. To convert a double-bed frame to queen size, have a machine shop or metal shop weld a 6-inch length of angle iron to each of the side rails. This accommodates the length of the mattress; the mattress width will overhang the frame by about 3 inches on each side, which won't show when the bed is made.

You don't have to limit your shopping to bed frames, however. Create your own distinctive headboard with a garden gate, a section of fancy iron fencing, pressed-tin ceiling panels, or a magnificent mantel. Or go a step further and assemble your own four-poster, using oars, old columns, or mix-and-match stair newels. A machine

Make one pair of bark cloth draperies work for two windows. Staple one long side of each panel across the top of the window frame. Catch up the center of the opposite side with a safety pin.

shop can attach the repurposed "posts" to a metal bed frame with sockets or braces. If you like to read in bed, attach the headboard securely to the wall so you can lean against it. Add plenty of plump pillows for comfort and back support.

Once you've established your style with your bed, make sure you like the view *from* the bed. Sit back and notice where your eye naturally rests. What do you see? An old wardrobe with a beautiful patina? Favorite paintings in flea market frames? Old-fashioned hatboxes covered with floral paper? Your bedroom can be a relaxing haven if you surround yourself with objects and images that please your eye and comfort your spirit.

Need storage? Vintage armoires and dressers can be a better buy than new furniture. You also can tuck clothes into hatboxes, trunks, and pie safes. A cupboard with shelves 12 inches deep and at least 5 inches apart can hold shoes, stacks of sweaters, or baskets of socks—and add personality to the room, too.

An old sewing machine cabinet, paired with a skinny mirror and gooseneck lamp, serves as a dressing table. The pie safe offers lots of storage. A tree branch makes a natural curtain rod.

❶ Create a bed you can't wait to crawl into with piles of plump pillows covered in vintage fabrics or soft cotton cases. Starting with a wonderful painted bed helps, of course, but even if your bed is more ho-hum, you can romance it—and your whole room—with layers of vintage fabrics. Spread lacy crocheted tablecloths over sheets or coverlets, toss a bark cloth spread across the end of the bed for color, and soften the windows with loose swags of bark cloth and lace. ❷ Give charming embroidered pieces new life by stitching them into small decorative pillows. ❸ Cover the shade of an old dresser lamp with chenille or dotted swiss and trim the edges with ball fringe for bedside lighting with old-fashioned appeal.

Be sure your ceilings are high enough before you fall in love with a magnificent bed like this. Referred to as cottage furniture, such pieces were mass-produced in the 19th century for workers' homes as well as the summer cottages of the wealthy.

making a vanity tray:

❶ Turn an old picture frame into a vanity tray by fitting it with a mirror. Have a glass company cut a piece of mirror to the required size. This 8x10-inch piece of mirror costs about $4.

❷ From a hardware store, buy glazing points (for installing glass panes in windows). Place the frame facedown on a sturdy work surface and lay the mirror in the opening.

Push the tip of a glazing point into the wood. Hold a square-blade screwdriver against the projecting tabs and tap it with a hammer to drive the point into the frame. Use at least three points on each side. To keep them from working out, place a drop of glue or epoxy at each point of entry.

1 This lyre-shaped frame has lost its washstand base, but turned upside down, it becomes a shapely quilt rack. It's mounted on the wall with sawtooth picture hangers. **2** Pressed-tin ceiling panels from an opera house cost the homeowners $40 at a flea market. The panels are attached to a wood frame that holds them away from the wall so they appear to float.

❶

❶ A wooden hospital gurney with metal legs made its way to Chicago from a Paris flea market to become a bathroom vanity. A hole cut in the silver-painted wooden top accommodates the sink; the faucet and handles are surface-mounted on the top of the gurney, so the unit can move with the homeowner. ❷ A cast-iron fireplace insert from a turn-of-the-century house performs butler duty beside a tub. (The piece also could go outdoors as a planter or chairside table; or, with the addition of a fabric-covered plywood top, it could make a sturdy

2

footstool.) The flower vase is a cast-iron soap dish turned on its back. The "legs" would have hooked around supports in the wall to hold

the dish in place. New rusted-look wire baskets are inexpensive at flea markets and can hold fresh towels indoors or plants outdoors. To

keep the rust from rubbing off on fabrics, spray the piece with several coats of matte-finish clear acrylic sealer (available from a crafts

store). The ubiquitous sap can holds sponges and bath supplies. An orchard ladder leaning against the wall makes a good towel rack.

❶ A silver pastry server offers soaps beside the sink. **❷** A diminutive spice rack displays toiletries and flowers in a romantic bathroom. **❸** This cast-iron cart with lid might have held cigarettes at one time. It's just right for cotton swabs in this bathroom, but it could travel to the kitchen to hold sugar packets, too. **❹** If you don't serve soup very often, use your tureen to serve fresh towels.

home offices

Whether your office is a separate room in the house or just a table with a computer tucked into a corner of the kitchen or den, make it comfortable, organized, and efficient with flea market finds.

Why buy a plywood desk with an imitation wood-grain finish when you can work at a farm table that has some real character and charm? Worn paint evokes layers of history and brings a feeling of soul to a room—and it's important to have a nurturing atmosphere when you're working, creating, or attending to a home-based business.

To have an office that's good for your body as well as your spirits, pay attention to ergonomics, too. The tabletop supporting a computer monitor and keyboard should be 24 to 27 inches above the floor and wide enough for the monitor to rest 18 to 24 inches away from you, slightly below eye level. Your worktable can be old, but your chair should be new and fully adjustable; you should be able to sit with your feet resting comfortably on the floor, your back well supported, and your arms bent at the elbow at a 90-degree angle to reach the keyboard. Office-supply stores sell padded wrist rests to place in front of the keyboard to give your arms and wrists extra support.

A wire basket holds fabric selections for an interior designer's client, and a narrow wooden box with dividers organizes office supplies and business cards. The table and guest chair are flea market finds as well.

1 Bowling balls drilled out and joined with a metal rod make unique legs for an office table created by designer Travis Smith. If you love license plates, show them off as wainscoting. Painting the top half of the walls a solid color balances the exuberant color and pattern. **2** Rusty cistern cups hang on the wall to organize office supplies; a chicken feeder sorts mail on the top of the secretary.

1 Artist Rick Singleton assembled this light fixture from building sets and die-cast trucks. He wired it so the insides of the trucks light up; halogen task lighting comes from the underside of the bridge. **2** Rick collects mid-20th-century machinery and transforms it into new accessories. An old-fashioned on-off switch combines with a traditional lamp top. **3** A pressure gauge and cash register serve as bookends; the bike chain is a lamp base.

gardens & patios

Outdoors is the obvious place to use architectural salvage and rusting furniture. Already mellowed by the elements, such treasures will be right at home. But why not go beyond the obvious?

Sure, old garden chairs provide a great front-row seat for watching fireflies at night, and wrought-iron tables were made for outdoor uses. But what about creating your own porch furniture from found objects—like the industrial-size shovel shown at left? Or consider using old doors, windows, and architectural pieces to make your deck or patio feel like a room with age and character. In this era of garden-style decorating, the boundaries are being blurred; it makes sense to bring as much comfort and style to your outdoor rooms as you would to your indoor ones.

If you have a standard privacy fence from a home improvement center, consider endowing it with some personality by layering a weathered door over it. The door need not cover an actual opening; the idea is to create a focal point and bring depth and texture to what may be a featureless wall. Add still more depth with plant hangers you can mount directly on the fencing; if you can find peeling-paint metal ones, so much the better.

1 Salvaged brackets and a window frame turn an arbor into an outdoor room. Metal sconces on the "door frame" hold candles. **2** Turn a feed tub from a farm-supply store into a water garden. Just install a submersible pump, available from hardware stores and garden-supply shops. You'll also need an outdoor electrical receptacle with a ground fault circuit interrupter (GFCI).

1

②

Even an arbor can feel like a more architecturally defined space if you add salvaged brackets to create an arched doorway and hang a window frame from the beam to suggest a wall enclosing the arbored room. Bring out comfortable, cushiony furniture, too. If you rely on wrought iron for the garden, consider stitching up some extra-plump pillows for the seats and backs of the chairs and settees. You'll need to bring the cushions in when it rains, but the greater comfort you'll enjoy will be worth it. Don't forget ottomans or footstools for the garden either. After all, you like to put your feet up indoors, don't you?

❷

❸

❶ Use flea market finds to place plants at different heights for a more interesting display. Look for unusual containers, too—colanders, pots, and kettles, for example—and add a horizontal element, such as a fallen pillar. ❷ If you don't like to sit on rust, clean and repaint the chair seat and back (see page 213 for tips). ❸ Bring a collection into the garden to personalize the space as you would a room indoors. Here, Stephen Rutledge's collection of orbs, from marbles to bowling balls, rolls into view (see his home on pages 70–77).

① Give your plants containers with character. A 1950s ice chest, bearing a painted folk-art design, blossoms with an exuberant collection of flowers. In wooden containers or those with no drainage holes, plant the flowers in plastic or terra-cotta pots with dishes to catch excess water, then place the pots in the flea market container. Use bricks, if necessary, to raise the flowers above the container's rim. **②** Fill a blue enameled pot with ice to keep drinks cold. **③** A blue-painted mail sorter found in an antiques shop holds a window-box assortment of flowers and foliage.

can it be saved?

Maybe your potential flea market prize just needs a good bath to remove the dust and grime. Or maybe it needs major surgery before you can use it. If it does require surgery, is it worth the price? Before you buy, be aware of what's involved in cleaning and restoration. This section offers basic guidelines for cleaning and reclaiming some of the most popular types of flea market finds for decorating.

cleaning
& care

Is that classic carved sofa worth the investment? Here are some guidelines to help you decide. You'll also find tips for cleaning wood, metals, glassware, and textiles.

upholstered pieces

If the shape of a sofa or chair appeals to you and the construction is sturdy, reupholstering can be a good investment. You'll need six to 10 yards of fabric for a chair and 12 to 20 yards for a sofa, depending on the fabric's pattern and the piece's shape and size. Labor may cost $250 to $700 for a chair and $1300 for a sofa, depending on where you live. To decide whether a piece is worth the expense, Chicago interior designer Jean Alan asks the following questions:

Is the piece heavy? If so, it's hardwood and probably well-constructed. If it's lightweight, it may be disposable.

Does it have an interesting shape? If it has a distinctive outline that isn't being reproduced by furniture manufacturers or a classic shape that never goes out of style, you'll have a piece that you couldn't just walk into a furniture store and buy.

What condition is it in? You can have springs retied and webbing replaced, and you can refinish scuffed or scratched woodwork. Missing veneer, however, can be

1 The stuffing has been pulled back to check the condition of the springs, which will be retied as needed to provide firm, comfortable seating.

2 This chair has been stripped back to the old kapok padding. The padding will be replaced with foam, which will be covered with batting before new fabric is applied.

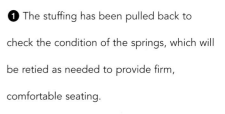

1 This frame just needs cleaning and waxing. For a good-as-new look, however, a restorer also could recarve the detail on the front foot and restain it. **2** A single seat cushion is a sign of an expensive sofa, and if it's squashy and easy to sink into, you know it's down-filled. The front edge of the sofa should compress easily so it will be comfortable to sit on. If the seat feels lumpy under the cushion, that simply means an upholsterer needs to retie the springs. **3** Know your woods. Walnut is good quality wood but softer than maple. On this piece, nice carving with lots of detail marks it as a fine sofa from the 1920s.

expensive and time consuming to replace. And if the back legs are broken, think twice. The back legs must bear the weight, and on a well-made sofa or chair, they are sturdy and splayed or slanted slightly back. Broken back legs are hard to fix satisfactorily.

Check underneath to see if the piece has tightly woven springs and webbing. If the springs are covered by fabric, feel for firmness.

chairs, tables, dressers

Check for broken parts, split wood, and insect holes. Powderpost beetles burrow into wood, leaving holes on the surface and little piles of wood powder beside the holes. You'll need to have an exterminator fumigate the piece for you. Otherwise, the beetles may begin munching on your other furniture. Spraying insecticide inside the holes is not likely to be effective, but you can try putting small wood items in the freezer for a couple of days or heating them in a microwave oven (if there are no metal parts) to kill the insects.

stained wood

A decade ago, almost everyone who bought old furniture stripped and refinished it as a matter of course. Today, there's a greater appreciation for the original surface, and refinishing can slash an antique's value dramatically. If you think you have something valuable, check with an antiques appraiser before you do anything.

how to apply paste wax:

1 Put a spoonful of wax (about the size of a golf ball) in a square of 100 percent cotton fabric. Wrap the fabric around the ball of wax and knead it until it's soft, then rub the fabric over the surface of the wood in a circular motion. Work on one small area at a time.

2 When the surface dulls, that means the solvents in the wax have evaporated, so it's time to wipe off the excess. Use a soft, clean cotton cloth, turning it frequently. If you can leave a streak with your finger, there's still too much wax on the surface, so you'll need to keep wiping. Repeat waxing and wiping until you've waxed the entire piece.

3 Polish the wood with a soft cloth or with a lamb's-wool pad attached to an electric drill or a power buffer. Smearing wax means there's *still* too much on the surface, and you'll need to rub more off before you continue buffing.

4 For an even deeper shine, apply a second coat of wax in the same way. To maintain waxed furniture, simply dust it with a lamb's-wool duster. Don't use liquid furniture polish because it will dissolve the wax. And don't use aerosol furniture polishes; they can eventually build up a hazy film.

Even if the piece isn't valuable, reviving the original finish with simple cleaning and waxing is the best way to retain its patina and charm. Use oil soap and water to wash off grime, then rinse and dry well. If the finish still seems dirty, go over it with No. 0000 steel wool dipped in naphtha. Apply clear paste wax, following the instructions on page 201.

An old recipe referred to as "furniture juice," a mixture of equal parts boiled linseed oil, turpentine, and white vinegar, once was recommended for cleaning and polishing wood furniture, and some dealers still use linseed oil. Museum conservators have since realized that the concoction darkens wood and locks onto dust, lint, and fingerprints like a magnet.

to refinish

If the finish is badly damaged, refinishing may be the answer. Furniture restoration and refinishing are an art, but even beginners can tackle simple jobs on inexpensive pieces. (If you have a valuable piece, however, it's best to take it to a professional.)

Hardware stores sell chemical strippers that remove almost any finish; these are toxic chemicals, so be sure to follow all of the manufacturer's instructions carefully. A more cautious approach calls for identifying the finish and using the appropriate solvent. This lets you melt the old finish to remove dirt and grime without lifting out the wood's color. In an inconspicuous spot, rub the surface with denatured alcohol. If the finish gets sticky, it's shellac and can be removed with alcohol. If denatured alcohol doesn't affect the finish, try turpentine. If the surface becomes sticky, it's varnish and can be removed with turpentine. If neither alcohol nor turpentine has an effect, try lacquer thinner, which

❶ Tiny paint specks marred the finish on this Moroccan inlaid table.

❷ To remove paint specks, rub with No. 0000 steel wool. Follow with a coat of paste wax, applied as directed on page 201.

can this piece be saved?

❶ Drawer glides that have broken away from the frame are easy to fix with carpenter's glue. Scrape off any old glue before applying new. If drawers stick, sand the bottom edges and the glides, and coat them with paste wax, or run a candle over them. ❷ If veneer has separated from the base, it can be reglued. Replacing missing veneer is a manageable job if the veneer is common, like this oak, and if you have some experience with woodworking. ❸ Caning that's laced through holes in the frame must be repaired by a professional. If the cane is a prewoven sheet that is splined into a groove around the frame, replacing it is an easy job for an amateur. ❹ Pull out the drawers to see what the wood is on a painted or "antiqued" piece. This avocado green antique glaze hides solid mahogany, as you can see on the drawer fronts; so the desk would be well worth stripping and refinishing.

❺ Minor wicker problems can be repaired, but you would have to strip the wicker on this baby buggy back to the frame and reweave it entirely—spot repairs wouldn't be possible. That could cost several hundred dollars, more than the buggy is worth.

removes lacquer. If none of these works, it may be polyurethane; use a methylene chloride-based finish remover. Be sure to work in a well-ventilated area and wear neoprene rubber gloves, a work apron, and goggles or other eye protection.

After removing the finish, wash the piece with a solution of two parts lacquer thinner to one part denatured alcohol to remove the residue. If the original finish was varnish, use naphtha instead of alcohol in the solution. Let the piece dry, then wipe clean with

denatured alcohol and apply the finish of your choice—varnish, lacquer, shellac, French polish, or paste wax.

painted furniture

Paint manufactured before 1978 probably contains lead. If the paint is in good condition and not flaking or cracking, it's not a health hazard, unless you have small children who may be tempted to chew on the item. Clean the piece with a sudsy solution of oil soap and water. Rinse and dry well, then apply clear paste wax.

If the paint finish is peeling, don't scrape it. That could generate lead-bearing dust, which poses a health hazard. Instead, use a hair dryer or heat gun set at 1100 degrees or lower to loosen the paint. Scrape off the loosened paint, misting the piece with water to control the dust, and wear a HEPA-filter respirator while you work. (Check with a hardware store for the respirator.) Cover your work area with plastic to catch the paint scrapings. Some states have specific requirements regarding lead waste disposal; to find out whether your state has a lead waste hotline, call the National Lead Information Center at 800/LEADFYI.

to remove a painted finish

Not all painted finishes are charming. If the piece is less than 150 years old, use a chemical paint remover to strip off the old paint, then refinish it as you like. If it's more than 150 years old, the paint may be milk paint;

how to remove a painted finish:

1 Follow the manufacturer's instructions and precautions carefully. Protect the floor with newspapers, and wear neoprene refinishing gloves to protect your hands. (Also wear long sleeves and goggles.) Use an inexpensive synthetic brush you won't mind throwing away, and pour the stripper into a metal container (not glass or plastic). If you're stripping a table or chair, stand the legs in pie pans to catch the dripping sludge. Apply a generous coat of stripper, but don't brush back and forth. After about 15 minutes, the paint should begin to bubble up.

2 Use a heavy-duty plastic scraper to lift off the old paint. If the paint resists, let the stripper work longer. If after another 15 minutes, scraping still doesn't reveal bare wood, apply more stripper.

3 On rounded edges, curved surfaces, and turned legs, use a finish-removing pad or medium-fine steel wool to remove the sludge. To get into crevices and corners or carved details, use a toothpick or toothbrush. Don't use metal or sharp-edged tools that could gouge the wood.

After you've removed the paint sludge, wash the piece down with a rag or fine steel wool soaked in the solvent recommended on the can of stripper. Lacquer thinner is most common. This removes any remaining paint and neutralizes the stripping action of the chemicals. Clear streaks that appear embedded in the grain indicate that the wood may have been sealed with shellac before the finish was applied. To remove this sealer coat, rub the surface with fine steel wool soaked in denatured alcohol.

To prepare the wood for the new finish, sand it with 100-grit sandpaper, followed by 150-grit, and for the smoothest finish, 220-grit. Change sandpaper often; worn-out paper will scratch the wood unevenly and result in uneven staining. Wipe off sanding dust with a tack cloth. Once you've achieved the degree of smoothness you want, don't wipe the wood with mineral spirits or water; this will raise the wood fibers, and you'll have to sand again. Apply the stain of your choice or leave the wood its natural color and seal it with lacquer, varnish, or paste wax.

since this makes the piece more valuable, think twice about removing it. To test for milk paint, rub ammonia in an inconspicuous spot to see if it removes the paint. (Be careful working with ammonia—it's a toxic chemical.)

vintage linens

Hold fabrics up to the light to check for worn spots, tears, broken threads, and holes. Very old laces or fabrics may tear if washed. Linens that you find at antiques fairs usually are already cleaned and pressed, but if you find a cache of fabrics at a garage sale or hidden away in an antiques shop, you'll probably want to clean them.

Test a piece of embroidery for color-fastness by gently dabbing the thread on the back of the piece with a damp white cloth. If no color comes off on the cloth, you can wash the piece safely. (If color does come off, you'll need to have the piece dry-cleaned.) You can machine-wash embroidered dresser scarves, pillowcases, hand towels, and table runners from the 1930s and 1940s if the fabric is not worn or fragile. Press them while they're still damp.

To clean fine linen or pieces with handmade lace, fringe, or crocheted edgings, presoak them for about 15 minutes in clear water to loosen dirt. Then gently swish the linens in warm water with a mild, nonabrasive, phosphate-free soap. Avoid using bleach because it can damage the fibers. Rinse the textiles at least twice in clear water to remove all the soap.

Old stains may be impossible to remove but you can try soaking the textile in an enzyme cleaner such as Biz or Axion, diluted with water, before laundering. Or add a nonchlorine bleach to the wash water. The old-fashioned method of bleaching white fabrics is to carefully rub lemon juice and salt over the stain, then hang or dry the piece in the sun.

Wash chenille in a washing machine and dry it in a dryer. If you need to iron it, lay

how to rewire a lamp:

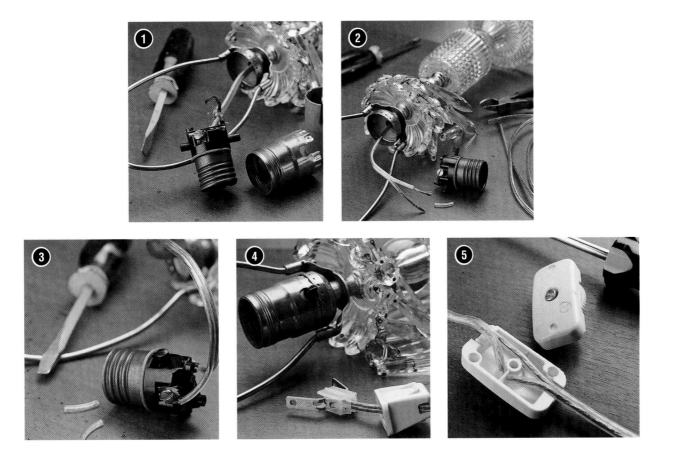

❶ Remove the metal socket cover by pressing near the switch (you'll see the word "press" engraved in the metal). Remove the cardboard liner and pull the socket out. Loosen the screws on the socket sides. Remove the old wire and pull the worn cord out of the lamp.

❷ Slide the new cord through the base of the lamp and out the socket end. With a utility knife, slit the plastic casing between the last 2 inches of cord, being careful not to cut the copper wires. Remove the plastic casing, exposing about an inch of wire.

❸ Twist the wires in one bundle, then wrap them around one socket screw, curling them in a clockwise

direction. Tighten the screw. Repeat for the other bundle of wires.

❹ Pull the wire from below until the socket rests securely on the top of the lamp. Replace the cardboard sleeve and snap the socket cover in place. To attach the plug, slide the blades out of the casing. Push the cord through the side of the casing and into the center of the blade piece. Squeeze the blades together and press the piece back into the casing.

❺ To add a new cord switch, unscrew the switch casing. Slit the plastic between the two wire bundles, and place one bundle along one side of the casing. Cut the other bundle and place as shown.

the fabric tufted side down on a well-padded ironing board and press, using the cotton setting.

Have draperies, bedding, or remnants of bark cloth professionally dry-cleaned. For these and other textiles that require dry cleaning (such as velvet or noncolorfast embroidery), look for a dry cleaner that uses the flat method rather than the tumble method; there's less abrasion and therefore less chance of damage to the fibers.

wicker

Wicker actually refers to the technique of bending and weaving a material such as paper, rattan, bamboo, or grasses. To clean dirty wicker that's made of bamboo, rattan, or willow, brush off or vacuum as much surface dirt as you can. Then wash it with a soft brush and soapy water to which you've added one or two teaspoons of ammonia. Rinse well and let the piece dry outdoors in the sun. To clean wicker made from twisted paper or grasses, simply wipe with a damp cloth.

To restore unpainted or natural wicker, rub it with linseed oil; wipe off the excess. Never paint antique natural wicker or you'll ruin the value.

leather

Clean leather upholstery by dusting or vacuuming. If necessary, wash with saddle soap, using as little water as possible. Buff the dry leather with a soft cloth. To

revive dry leather, use a commercial leather conditioner from a furniture store.

A home remedy for reconditioning leather calls for washing it with a solution of 1 teaspoon of household ammonia and 4 teaspoons of vinegar mixed with 2 cups of water. Dry, then wipe on castor oil, using a soft cloth. After the leather dries, rub on a leather shoe cream in the appropriate color and buff well to remove excess cream. This treatment would be more practical for small projects, such as a footstool or the seat of a side chair,

than for a sofa or club chair. Keep leather away from heat sources to prevent its drying out.

glassware and porcelain

Wash glassware in warm, soapy water. Remove the whitish film at the water line with vinegar. If dirt and grime have clouded the bottom of a glass vase or if the vase is stained, place some clean sand in the vase; add dish-washing liquid and warm water and swirl the sand around to dislodge the dirt. Let it stand overnight, then shake well and rinse. If the glass remains cloudy, fill it with water and add a denture-cleaning tablet.

Wash china and ceramics in warm, not hot, soapy water, and dry carefully with a soft linen towel. Don't use abrasives such as scouring powders.

silver and silverplate

Exposure to air turns silver black. Use a commercial silver polish according to the manufacturer's instructions, following the precautions carefully. Too much polishing eventually ruins silver and can remove silverplate completely. Never polish silver gilt because it will remove the gilding. Wear cotton gloves when cleaning or handling silver (or any other metal); the acid in your skin can tarnish or spot the metal. Antique silver should be cleaned professionally.

brass

To clean tarnished or corroded brass, use a commercial brass polish, following the manufacturer's instructions. Avoid cleaners that contain acids or chlorides, because these actually can cause new

corrosion. Don't polish lacquered brass; simply wash it occasionally in soapy water.

bronze

This alloy of copper and tin weathers to a warm brown or acquires a green coating called verdigris, the result of a reaction between the copper and chemicals in the atmosphere. (Copper and brass also may develop this deposit.) Have antique bronze cleaned professionally; washing can cause "bronze disease," or flaking metal. To remove verdigris, scrape carefully and gently with a knife, or brush with a dry toothbrush.

copper

Use a commercially available nonabrasive metal cleaner and polish recommended for copper. Home remedies—a lemon cut in half and dipped in salt or a paste made from salt, vinegar, and flour—remove tarnish instantly and leave the metal a bright copper color, but they also scratch and dull the surface.

iron

Exposure to air and moisture causes iron to rust. The color of the rust can be a clue to the object's age: orange rust is new. A deep brown rust has been forming over a long period of time. If you like the rusted look but you don't want rust rubbing off on everything it touches, try spraying the piece with clear lacquer from the hardware store or a matte clear acrylic sealer from a crafts store. This isn't a permanent solution: The rust will eventually "eat" through the sealer, and you'll need to reapply. If you like the color of

To clean cast iron that will be used to cook or serve food, remove rust with coarse salt and wash the piece in hot, soapy water. Rinse and dry well, then rub vegetable oil over all surfaces. To season a cast-iron pan to keep food from sticking and rust from forming, rub a thin coat of vegetable oil over the interior and place the pan in a 325- to 350-degree oven for two hours. Let the pan cool, wipe off the excess oil, rinse, and dry the pan.

steel

Because steel contains iron, it also will rust unless the surface has been protected with a lacquered finish. If the lacquered finish is intact, wash with soapy water, but avoid abrasives because they'll scratch the finish. Remove rust with an abrasive wheel or wire brush attached to an electric drill. If you want a trendy brushed-metal look, buff the bare metal with a wire wheel attached to an electric drill. (Be sure to wear eye protection when you do this.) For a more highly polished finish, use a buffing wheel and a polishing compound. Then protect the surface with clear paste wax, clear lacquer, or polyurethane.

Clean chrome-plated tubular steel with a chrome/aluminum polish or rubbing compound, found in the automotive section of a discount or hardware store. Apply a light coat of silicone furniture polish to protect the shine.

rust but not the mess, clean the metal, then prime it with a rust-color primer and top with a clear enamel spray. (See also page 112.)

To remove rust entirely, use a wire brush or an abrasive wheel attached to an electric drill. You can remove rust on small decorative metal items with fine steel wool dipped in mineral spirits or vinegar and water; protect the surface with a coat of paste wax.

how to refinish painted metal:

1 To remove old paint from metal furniture, use a chemical paint remover. To get down to bare metal, you may need to scrub with a wire brush, followed by steel wool, and finally, an electric sander. Be sure to wear a protective mask and goggles.

2 To repaint the piece, first apply a primer to neutralize further oxidation and to give the paint a surface to which it can adhere. The right primer depends on the type of metal. For galvanized iron or steel, look for zinc-oxide or a primer labeled for use on galvanized metal. Zinc-oxide also works on aluminum. Also check the label to be sure your primer and top coat are compatible; otherwise the top coat may not adhere.

3 After the primer dries, apply a fast-drying acrylic enamel. Instead of a single thick coat, which will drip and run, use two or three thin coats, letting the paint dry between applications.

If you like the look of rusting, peeling painted metal like the bar stools and cast-iron tub feet above, simply brush off the loose paint. If you prefer a good-as-new look, strip the piece and then prime and paint it with an enamel designed for metals.

antiques shows & flea markets

If you like to make antiquing part of your vacation travels, consider including the following shows in your plans. There's something for everyone, from old-fashioned trade days to high-end antiques shows. Please note that the information included here was correct at press time but may have changed since publication.

Alabama

Scottsboro: FIRST MONDAY TRADE DAYS, year-round, the first Monday of the month and the preceding weekend. Since the 1850s, people have come to the square around the courthouse to swap and trade. Free admission. Call 800/259-5508 for more information.

California

San Francisco: TREASURE ISLAND FLEA MARKET, Sundays year-round. 100 to 150 vendors. Parking free; admission $2. The market is open from 6 a.m. to 4 p.m., but some dealers start to pack up around 2 p.m. Call 415/255-1923 for more information, or check www.treasureislandmarket.com.

Pasadena: ROSE BOWL FLEA MARKET AND SWAP MEET, year-round, second Sunday of the month. 2,200 dealers. Admission: preview/VIP, 6 a.m. to 7:30 a.m., $15; early, 7:30 a.m. to 9 a.m., $10; general, 9 a.m. to 3 p.m. $5. Call 323/560-7469 for directions and more information.

Connecticut

Farmington: FARMINGTON ANTIQUES WEEKEND, second weekend in June and Labor Day weekend. About 600 dealers offer everything from formal furniture to country pieces, sterling silver, and prints; no reproductions, no new merchandise. Admission: early buyer, Saturday, 7 a.m. to 10 p.m., $25; general, 10 a.m. to 5 p.m., $5. Saturday admission includes free pass for Sunday; ask at the ticket booth. Call 800/494-0051 for directions, or to receive a brochure, e-mail Revival Promotions at www.farmington-antiques.com.

Florida

Mt. Dora: RENNINGERS FLORIDA TWIN MARKETS, 20 miles north of Orlando; open year-round with three-day extravaganzas in January, February, and November. 1,400 dealers from around the country. Admission: early buyer (Friday), $10; general, Saturday 8 a.m. to 5 p.m., $5; Sunday 8 a.m. to 4 p.m., $3. Call 800/522-3555 for more information.

Georgia

Atlanta: LAKEWOOD ANTIQUES MARKET, south of the city on I-75. Year-round, second weekend of the month. 1,500 dealers. Admission: early (Thursday), $5; Friday, Saturday, and Sunday, $3. Free parking. Call 404/622-4488 for directions.

Illinois

Sandwich: SANDWICH ANTIQUES MARKET, U.S. 34, 60 miles southwest of Chicago. One Sunday a month, usually the third or fourth weekend,

May through October; call 815/786-3337 for exact dates. 600 dealers indoors and out. Admission: $5, children under 12 free.

Grayslake: GRAYSLAKE ANTIQUES, COLLECTIBLES AND FLEA MARKET AT THE FAIRGROUNDS, second Sunday of the month year-round. 350 antiques dealers in four buildings; flea market runs concurrently outdoors. Admission: early, 6:30 a.m., $15; general, 8 a.m., $4. The market closes at 3 p.m. Call 847/223-2204 for more information.

St. Charles: KANE COUNTY FLEA MARKET, Kane County Fairgrounds, 35 miles west of Chicago. Year-round, the first Saturday of the month (12 noon to 5 p.m.) and Sunday (7 a.m. to 4 p.m.). 600 dealers in winter months, up to 1,500 in summer. Admission: $5; children and parking free. Call 630/377-2252 for more information.

Iowa

Des Moines: HISTORIC VALLEY JUNCTION ANTIQUES JAMBOREE, second Sunday of June, August, and

September, 8 a.m. to 5 p.m. 150 vendors from around the Midwest. Free admission, free parking. Call 515/222-3642 for more information.

What Cheer: COLLECTOR'S PARADISE FLEA MARKET, INC., at the Fairgrounds, 20 miles south of I-80 on Highway 21. First weekend in May, August, and October. 300 to 500 dealers. Admission: $2 early (Friday), $1 Saturday and Sunday. Opens at 7 a.m. Call 515/634-2109 for more information.

Kentucky

Mount Sterling: OCTOBER COURT DAYS, I-64 east of Lexington, west of Ashland; the third Monday in October and the preceding weekend. Old-fashioned trade days. Free admission. Call the Chamber of Commerce for details, 606/498-5343.

Maryland

West Friendship: MID-ATLANTIC ANTIQUES MARKET, Howard County Fairgrounds, west of Baltimore. Last Sunday in March and October; 120 exhibitors from all over the country.

Admission: early, 7:30 a.m., $15; general, 9 a.m., $6. Call Sims Rogers at 410/228-8858 for more information.

Massachusetts

Brimfield: BRIMFIELD OUTDOOR ANTIQUES AND COLLECTIBLES SHOW, Route 20, 1 hour from Boston; held in May, July, and September, Tuesday through Sunday. Call 413/283-6149 for dates, directions, and a schedule of events during the week. The show covers several fields; most are free, but some charge $5 admission.

Rowley: TODD'S FARM FLEA MARKET AND ANTIQUES, on Route 1-A, Main Street; 13 antiques shops open year-round, flea market open on Sundays, April to Thanksgiving. 225 dealers. Free admission, free parking. Dealers and buyers arrive as early as 3 a.m. Market closes at 4 p.m., but dealers may leave earlier. Call 978/948-3300 for details.

Michigan

Allegan: ALLEGAN ANTIQUES MARKET, about 50 miles south of Grand Rapids, last Sunday of the month, April

through September. 400 dealers. Admission: early (Saturday), $30; general, $3. Call 616/735-3333 for directions and more information.

Missouri

Greenwood: ANTIQUES ON THE COMMON, southeast of Kansas City. 65 dealers plus established shops featuring country antiques. One-day show in May and September. Admission: early, 8 a.m. to 4 p.m., $9; general, 10 a.m. to 8 p.m., $4. For directions and information, call Claire Fellows, Country Heritage Promotions, 816/537-7822.

New Hampshire

Manchester: ANTIQUES WEEK IN NEW HAMPSHIRE, the week after the first Saturday in August. A series of shows featuring Americana, folk art, and country antiques opens during the week. Each charges an admission fee of about $8. No early buyer admissions, but opening hours are staggered. Call 207/767-3967 for directions and schedule.

New Jersey

Atlantic City: "ATLANTIQUE CITY HOLIDAY MEGAFAIR—THE LARGEST INDOOR ART, ANTIQUE, AND COLLECTIBLES SHOW IN THE WORLD." March and October. 1,600 dealers in 10½ indoor acres, includes dealers from 41 states plus Canada, Europe, and the Far East. Admission: advance-purchase tickets cost less than if you buy at the box office, and one- or two-day passes are also available. Call 800/526-2724 for a courtesy pack with early entry tickets and hotel and airline discounts.

New Mexico

Santa Fe: SANTA FE ANTIQUES SHOW, at the Sweeney Convention Center, July 4th weekend and December 27-29. 100 dealers. Admission: $7.50 per day or $12 for a two-day pass. Call 505/753-2553.

New York

New York City: ANNEX ANTIQUES FAIR AND FLEA MARKET, 6th Avenue at 26th Street; year-round, Saturday and Sunday, sunrise to sunset. Admission $1 at one location, others free. Call 212/243-5343.

SOHO ANTIQUES FAIR, on the corner of Broadway and Grand Street, two blocks north of Canal Street; Saturday and Sunday year-round, 9 a.m. to 5 p.m. 50 to 100 vendors offer a variety of antiques and imported handcrafts. Call 212/682-2000 for information.

Rhinebeck: RHINEBECK ANTIQUES FAIR at the county fairgrounds. Memorial Day weekend (observed), fourth Saturday in July, and Columbus Day weekend (observed). 190 dealers offering high-quality antiques, period English and French furniture, vintage textiles, Staffordshire, and country painted furniture. Admission: $7 in May and October, $6 in July. Call 914/876-1989 for information.

North Carolina

Charlotte: GREAT AMERICAN ANTIQUES SPECTACULAR, off I-77, exit 16A east on Sunset Road. Held in April, June, and November on the first Saturday of the month and the preceding Friday, 8 a.m. to 5 p.m.; Sunday, 9 a.m. to 5 p.m. Indoors and out, 6,000 dealers (4,000 in June) offer antiques and antique collectibles from around the world. Smaller shows are held in the remaining months. Call 704/596-4643 or 800/824-3770 for details.

Pennsylvania

Adamstown: RENNINGER'S ANTIQUE MARKET, year-round, Sundays 7:30 a.m. to 5 p.m. Extravaganza weekends, last weekend in April, June, and September. 700 dealers indoors and out. Free admission. Call 717/336-2177 for more information.

Kutztown: RENNINGER'S ANTIQUES, COLLECTIBLES, AND FARMER'S MARKET, south of Allentown. Extravaganzas, last full weekend in April, June, and September. Admission: early buyers (Thursday) 10 a.m. to 5 p.m., $40 per car (one to three passengers; the pass is good for all three days); general admission Friday, 7 a.m. to 6 p.m., $6; Saturday, 7 a.m. to 5 p.m., $4. Call 877/385-0104 for directions, or check the website, www.renningers.com.

Tennessee

Nashville: HEART OF COUNTRY, held at the Opryland Hotel in mid-February and mid-October. A must-see three and one-half day event for country-antiques collectors. 150 to 200 dealers. Preview party ($60) includes early-buying opportunity, dinner, music, and free admission for the rest of the show. General admission $8. For brochure and special hotel rates, call 800/862-1090 or visit the website, www.heartofcountry.com.

Texas

Canton: FIRST MONDAY TRADE DAYS, year-round, Thursday through Sunday before the first Monday of the month. More than 4,000 dealers on 100 acres plus indoor antiques and collectibles market. Free admission; parking costs $3. Off I-20, 55 miles east of Dallas. Call 903/567-6556.

Round Top: Although the antiques show that made this little town in the Texas Hill Country famous aims at museum curators and high-end collectors of country antiques, several other markets take place around the same time in late May to early April and late September to early October. Call the Chamber of Commerce at 409/249-4042 for dates or request a brochure from their website at www.roundtop.org.

Virginia

Oatlands Plantation, 6 miles south of Leesburg: OATLANDS HUNT COUNTRY ANTIQUE FAIR, January, April, and September. 200 dealers offering a broad array of antiques. Admission $5. Call 703/777-3174 for dates and directions.

Richmond: THE RICHMOND ANTIQUES SPECTACULAR, at The Showplace on Route 360 East (exit 192 off I-64). Held one weekend a month in January, February, March, June, September, and November, 10 a.m. to 6 p.m. on Saturday, noon to 5 p.m. on Sunday. 225 dealers offer 18th- and 19th-century European and American furniture, Art Deco, Art Moderne, "smalls," porcelain, jewelry, books, and more. Admission $3 per day. Call 804/462-6190 for more information.

Outside the United States

Because the locations of local flea markets and antiques shows change often, Barbara Novogratz (see pages 40–47) suggests asking the concierge of your hotel for recommendations; or call the tourist council when you arrive. Some well established European markets include:

In **London,** the BERMONDSEY ANTIQUE MARKET every Friday; the PORTOBELLO

ROAD FLEA MARKET every Saturday; and the CAMDEN PASSAGE ANTIQUE MARKETS, Islington, every Saturday. In **Paris,** check out the ANTIQUE FLEA MARKET AT PORTE DE CLIGANCOURT, held every Saturday, Sunday, and Monday year-round; and PORTE DE VANVES, Saturday and Sunday year-round. SAINT-OUEN, on the north side of Paris, features 3,000 booths. METZ, a three-hour drive from Paris, has a notable flea market on the first and third Saturday of the month,

except in August. NANCY has a flea market on the first and third Wednesdays of the month.

In **Canada**, check out the following: HARBOURFRONT ANTIQUE MARKET at 390 Queens Quay West, Toronto, open Tuesday through Sunday; 416/260-2626. WATERLOO COUNTY ANTIQUE WAREHOUSE, next to St. Jacob's Farmers Market on Regional Road 15 in St. Jacob's, Ontario, open daily; 888/843-9929. In British Columbia, the VILLAGE ANTIQUES & CRAFT MALL at 23331 Mavis St., Ft. Langley, open Tuesday through Sunday; 604/888-3700. VICTORIA FLEA MARKET at 3400 Tillicum Road, Victoria; 250/652-8259.

Additional helpful resources

Books *The Official Directory to U.S. Flea Markets* (6th edition), published by House of Collectibles, 1998; *The Official Price Guide to Flea Market Treasures* (5th edition) by Harry L. Rinker, Jr., and published by House of Collectibles, 1999; *Flea* by Sheila Zubrod & David Stern,

HarperPerennial, 1997.

The Internet For a state-by-state listing of U.S. flea markets, check out www.FleaMarketGuide.com. Although it is geared to vendors, it includes useful information for buyers, too. For a directory of collectors' clubs and societies, try www.collectoronline.com.

In addition to auction sites such as eBay, eHammer, and Amazon.com, you can shop for antiques and collectibles by visiting sites such as www.tias.com. Vendors with websites accessed through tias.com generally offer a money-back guarantee if you're not satisfied with the merchandise, so it's a lot like shopping by catalog.

Because listings on the Internet are constantly changing, the best way to find the most current information is to choose a search engine such as Hotbot, AltaVista, Lycos, Google, or Excite, and type in "flea markets" or "antiques"; or type in the country you want to visit and look under "shopping" or "antiques."

resources & contributors

South

Jeff Jones
310 9th Street
Atlanta, GA 30309
404/876-4574
jjdzn@mindspring.com
Pages 26–39

The Old Lucketts Store
42350 Lucketts Road
Leesburg, VA 20175
703/779-0268
Pages 152–53, 172–73

Twig House
132 Maple Avenue East
Vienna, VA 22180
703/255-4985
Pages 12, 14, 18, 139 left, 174

Northeast

Abodeon
1731 Massachusetts Ave.
Cambridge, MA 02138
617/497-0137

Greg Cann/CannDesigns
450 Harrison Ave., Studio 417
Boston, MA 02118
Page 124

Studio F.KIA
(Marcel Albanese)
617/357-5859
Pages 78–89

Fresh Eggs
58 Clarenden St.
Boston, MA 02116
617/247-8150

Rick Singleton
Visionary Lighting
4840 MacArthur Blvd. #104
Washington, D.C. 20007
301/986-9680
rsin11@aol.com
Pages 137, 165 right,
186–87

**Travis Smith/Good Eye 20th
Century Interiors**
4918 Wisconsin Ave. NW
Washington, D.C. 20016
202/244-8516
www.goodeyeonline.com
Pages 149, 184

Midwest

**Jean Alan Upholstered
Furniture and Furnishings**
2134 North Damen
Chicago, IL 60647
773/278-2345
Pages 122–23, 128

**Bernacki & Associates,
Inc./Oakley Interiors**
(Restoration, conservation, to
the trade only)
424 North Oakley Blvd.
Chicago, IL 60612
312/243-5669
Pages 198, 199

Lakeside Depot
14906 Red Arrow Highway
Lakeside, MI 49116
616/469-9700
Pages 194–95

Peg Shulha, interior
decorator; 630/554-5590
Pages 150, 154, 158–61, 163

C. J. VanDaff
**VanDaff's Interior Design
and Antiquities**
2120 Wealthy SE
East Grand Rapids, MI 49506
616/456-0532
Pages 48–61, 183

West Coast

Intérieur Perdu
340 Bryant
San Francisco, CA 94107
415/543-1616
Pages 104–117

**Joseph Ruggiero &
Associates**
www.ruggieroideas.com
Pages 127, 132–33, 134,
138, 144, 185 right

Zonal Home Interiors
2139 Polk Street
San Francisco, CA 94109
415/563-2220
www.zonalhome.com
Pages 131, 140 left, 141
right, 189

Thanks to **Larry Johnston** and
Bill Krier, *Wood* Magazine,
for their expertise, and to
**Thea Beasley, Suzanne
Eblen, Esther Fishman,
Debbie Heagy, Dr. Rebecca
Roberts,** and **Darva Murray**
for sharing their homes and
creativity.

Photo and styling credits

All photography by **Bill Holt**
except the following:

King Au, pages 129, 175,
176, 202 inset

Marty Baldwin, page 201

Jon Bessler, pages 6, 10, 16,
17, 19, 20, 21 left, 25, 120,
130 right, 197, 204, 209

Randy Foulds, pages 148,
170, 177

Hopkins Associates, pages
205, 207

Jon Jenson, page 180;
(interior designers, **Judy
Simes,** ASID, and **Dick
Kenarney**); 181 right

Jenifer Jordan, page 121;
126 (produced by **Nancy E.
Ingram**)

Mark Lohman Photography,
pages 127, 132–33, 134, 135
right, 138, 144, 185, 206

Eric Roth, page 124 (field
editor, **Estelle Bond
Guralnick**)

Dean Tanner, page 203

James Yochum Photography,
pages 194 left, 195

Jody T. Kennedy, styling on
pages 104–117, 131, 140
left, 141 right, 189

index